曹志建◎著

功能主义视角下的法律外宣文本翻译

On the Translation of Legal Texts for International Communication Purposes: a Functionalist Perspective

暨南大学出版社
JINAN UNIVERSITY PRESS
中国·广州

图书在版编目（CIP）数据

功能主义视角下的法律外宣文本翻译 = On the Translation of Legal Texts for International Communication Purposes：A Functionalist Perspective/曹志建著. —广州：暨南大学出版社，2016. 7

ISBN 978 - 7 - 5668 - 1874 - 4

Ⅰ. ①功…　Ⅱ. ①曹…　Ⅲ. ①法律—翻译—研究　Ⅳ. ①D90 - 055

中国版本图书馆 CIP 数据核字（2016）第 131252 号

功能主义视角下的法律外宣文本翻译
GONGNENG ZHUYI SHIJIAO XIA DE FALU WAIXUAN WENBEN FANYI
著者：曹志建

....

出 版 人： 徐义雄
责任编辑： 苏彩桃　黄燕红
责任校对： 周海燕
责任印制： 汤慧君　王雅琪

出版发行： 暨南大学出版社（510630）
电　　话： 总编室（8620）85221601
营销部（8620）85225284　85228291　85228292（邮购）
传　　真：（8620）85221583（办公室）　85223774（营销部）
网　　址： http：//www. jnupress. com　http：//press. jnu. edu. cn
排　　版： 广州市天河星辰文化发展部照排中心
印　　刷： 佛山市浩文彩色印刷有限公司
开　　本： 787mm × 960mm　1/16
印　　张： 10
字　　数： 210 千
版　　次： 2016 年 7 月第 1 版
印　　次： 2016 年 7 月第 1 次
定　　价： 30. 00 元

前　言

改革开放以来，中国在经济社会发展和法制建设领域取得了长足的进步，但西方世界对于我国司法体制的观感依然极为负面。究其原因，一方面是西方媒体对我国法制仍是一边倒的负面报道；另一方面则是我国司法外宣工作成效不大，效果欠佳。

有鉴于此，本书分析了我国司法外宣的现状，提出我国司法外宣成效之所以不理想，一方面是因为在外宣中过于强调对法律法规文件等硬性法律文本的翻译介绍，导致受众广大、更易于为受众接受的软性法律文本，例如以法律为主题的新闻报道或文学作品的翻译遭到边缘化，没有得到应有的重视，从而导致我国司法外宣的受众面非常狭窄，成效不明显；另一方面则是因为现阶段我国司法外宣文本的译文质量不佳，甚至令受众不知所云，更遑论争取受众的理解与支持，因而也就难以实现向世界客观公正地介绍中国司法现状的外宣目的。有鉴于此，本书选取我国司法外宣中软性法律文本的翻译（以下简称“司法外宣翻译”）作为研究对象，系统地分析我国司法外宣翻译中存在的问题及其成因，并在德国功能主义学派提出的翻译理论的基础上，初步提出了提高我国司法外宣翻译质量的解决方案。

本书在对相关文献进行回顾之后发现，一方面，虽然目前关于中国法律对外译介的研究虽日渐增多，但均以硬性法律文本的翻译为研究对象，并未涉及软性法律文本的翻译；另一方面，虽然目前外宣翻译在国内日益受到重视，但截至本书出版之时，国内还没有以我国法律体系为主题的外宣翻译研究。

因此，本书以德国功能学派提出的功能主义翻译理论，特别是“目的论”作为主要理论依据。原因在于功能主义翻译理论与我国几代从事外宣翻译的译员、记者、编辑和管理人员在多年经验之上总结的翻译规则和规律高度契合。在此基础上，本书对我国司法外宣翻译进行了分析，提出我国司法外宣翻译工作的目的在于以客观公正的方式向目标受众提供关于中国法律体系的信息，从而改变他们对中国法律体系的误解，消除西方媒体片面报道所带来的消极后果。我国司法外宣翻译译文的功能主要为信息功能，兼有委婉的诉求功能，因此，我国司法外宣翻译应属于以目标受众为中心，以符合目标受众所在文化中的文化规约和语言规则为特征的工具型翻译。

就此，本书提出，我国司法外宣翻译中普遍存在三类问题：语用翻译问题、文化翻译问题和语言翻译问题，并依据我国司法外宣翻译的目的和译文功能提出我国司法外宣翻译工作应采用“自上而下”的功能主义途径：以翻译纲要为基础，通过分析比较原文作者与接收者之间的交际情景和译文作者与译文接收者之间的交际场景上存在的差异，预先发现翻译可能遇到的问题，采用“工具型翻译”策略，在“辅助文本”的帮助下，按照“语用翻译问题”“文化翻译问题”和“语言翻译问题”的顺序，“自上而下”地解决翻译中出现的问题，使译文符合目标文本所在文化中的文化规约、规范以及语言规则，从而使译文能够符合目标受众的心理，满足目标受众的信息需求。

最后本书得出结论，重申了我国司法外宣翻译工作要以“实现翻译目的”作为中心，并指出了在现有条件下本书存在的不足，也对日后的研究工作进行了展望。

在我国经济取得举世瞩目的发展，国际地位大大提高，积极推进“走出去”战略的当代，以介绍中国国情、促进中外交流为首要目的的外宣翻译实践与理论研究大有可为。在这方面，本书仅仅是作者不顾浅陋而进行的极其微小的一次尝试。鉴于作者水平有限，敬请大家指正。

曹志建

2016 年 4 月

Contents

Chapter One Introduction

1.1 Background of the Present Research

Since it started to implement the policy of reform and opening-up at the end of the late 1970s, China has made enormous achievements in its social and economic development. In a relatively short span of just over thirty years, the economy of China has expanded by approximately eighteen times in the real GDP (gross domestic product) terms (Morrison, 2011: 1), while its Human Development Index (HDI), a key indicator of human welfare of a country, has risen from the level of 0.530 before the reform and opening-up to 0.777 in 2005, recording an "impressive" growth of over 30% (Tisdell, 2009) in less than three decades; China's economy has been growing at an annual rate three times of the world's average in the thirty years since the year of 1978 (Wearden, 2010); China has overtaken Japan to become the second largest economy of the world and in the process has lifted over 600 million of its citizens out of poverty, which is considered as "an achievement of staggering proportions"① by the United Nations.

Accompanying such phenomenal achievements in the era of globalization is a rapid increase in the flow of goods, services and personnel into and out of China. According to the government white paper released by the Information Office of the State Council of China in 2011, "by the end of 2010 China had been the world's largest exporter and second-largest importer for two consecutive years"②, only less than those after China's accession to the World Trade Organization (WTO)

---

① *China's Progress towards the Millennium Development Goals 2008 Report*, jointly released by the Ministry of Foreign Affairs of the People's Republic of China and the United Nations System in China (p.6).

② *China's Foreign Trade* (《中国的对外贸易》) is the first ever government white paper on foreign trade of China, which was released by the Information Office of the State Council on December, 2011. The text quoted in the present book is retrieved from the official website of *China Daily*, the largest English-language newspaper on the mainland of China at http://www.chinadaily.com.cn/china/2011-12/07/content_14226654_3.htm.

in 2001. According to the 2011 edition of *UNWTO Tourism Highlights*, the annual review reported by the World Tourism Organization on the development of international tourism industry, China became the third most popular tourist destination of the world in the year of 2010, receiving a total of 55.7 million international tourist arrivals and garnering $45.8 billion in revenue①. In addition, the results of the sixth national population census of China in 2010, the latest of its kind, showed that a total of 201,955 foreign nationals were working on the mainland of China. That demographic figure represented an estimated expat community of 1.02 million in China②; and finally, according to the annual work report of the Supreme People's Court (which is the highest court of law in China) made before the annual session of National People's Congress, China's national parliament, in March 2011, courts on the mainland of China heard and concluded as many as 20,258 commercial, marine and maritime cases involving foreign individuals and/or entities in the year of 2010 alone. To sum up, with China emerging as an important player on the international arena and the integration of China into the international community, the exchanges and interactions between China and the rest of the world have been expanding rapidly, and it is safe to assume that there is increasing interest and urgent practical need of a proper understanding of China, including its legal system, i.e., the laws, administrative regulations and other regulatory documents and the interpretation and enforcement thereof, which affects almost all aspects of such exchanges and interactions.

On the other hand, since the end of the chaotic years of the Cultural Revolution in the late 1970s, China has made enormous achievements in restoring its legal system and promoting the rule of law. China "has made remarkable progress in introducing a fully functioning civil law system" (Dickinson, 2007), while in the year of 1978, when China started to implement the policy of reform and opening-up, China had two laws only, namely, *the Constitution of the*

---

① *UNWTO Tourism Highlights* (2011 *Edition*), retrieved from the official website of the World Trade Organizations at http://mkt.unwto.org/sites/all/files/docpdf/unwtohighlights11enhr.pdf (pp. 5 - 6).

② The figures were released by the National Bureau of Statistics of China, the Chinese governmental agency in charge of the collection and publication of statistics related to the economy, population and society of China, and were quoted in a report titled "Legal cases involving foreign workers on the rise" posted on the website of *the Global Times*, an English-language newspaper of China.

People's Republic of China and *the Marriage Law of the People's Republic of China*, due to the damages inflicted on the legal system of China by the chaotic Cultural Revolution. A little more than three decades later, China has established a fairly well-developed legal system on the ruins of a decade of chaos, with the National People's Congress, China's top legislature and its standing committee adopting a total of 239 national laws, 14 judicial interpretations and decisions related to legal issues (侯瑞丽, 2011), to say nothing of any local laws, administrative regulations and other legislations and enactments adopted by local legislatures of the country. With the promulgation of new laws and regulations and amendments to the existing ones, China "is increasingly governed on the basis of publicly promulgated laws" (Peerenboom, 2003). "Even in the eyes of its harshest critics, China's legal system has come a long way in just over twenty years. Two decades of reform has brought remarkable changes in institutions, laws, and practices." (Peereboom, 2003)

However, in spite of the rising profile of China in the world, the phenomenal growth in the exchanges between China and the international community, and the leaps and bounds made by China in promoting the rule of law, the legal system of China remains unfortunately little known by the rest of the world, and the international community's understanding of China's legal system is sketchy, to say the least. As a matter of fact, China was obliged to make a commitment to the World Trade Organization upon its accession to the international trade body in 2001 that it would make transparent to all WTO members its national and local laws, administrative regulations and other measures, especially those "pertaining to or affecting trade in goods, services, trade-related aspects of intellectual property rights (TRIPS) or the control of foreign exchange"①. To fulfill this obligation, China should make available to all WTO members, upon request, all its trade-related laws, administrative regulations and other measures before such laws, administrative regulations and measures are implemented or enforced. In addition, China is also required to publish all trade laws and regulations and to provide a reasonable period for public comment to the appropriate authorities be-

① *Protocol on the Accession of the People's Republic of China*, retrieved from the website of the United Nations at http://unpan1.un.org/intradoc/groups/public/documents/APCITY/UNPAN002123.pdf (p. 2).

fore they are implemented. And most significantly, China should translate all such laws, administrative regulations and measures into at least one of the three official languages of the WTO, namely, English, French and Spanish, and make such translation available to all WTO members no later than 90 days after their implementation or enforcement (Qin, 2003). These unprecedented and unique requirements, which are exclusively applicable to the mainland of China (Wu, 2011), underscore the fact that there is an urgent need for knowledge about the legal system of China rendered in internationally accessible languages and that such knowledge is unfortunately in short supply.

What is worse, in spite of all the achievements made by China in improving its legal system, the perception of China's legal system by the international community is still "overwhelmingly and exceedingly negative" (Peerenboom, 2003). Much to the chagrin of those foreign nationals practicing law in China, there still remain some popularly held myths about the current legal system of China, which range from the outdated to the absurd—Myth No. 1: There are no laws in China; Myth No. 2: There are few lawyers in China and they are poorly educated; Myth No. 3: There are few judges in the Middle Kingdom and they are poorly educated; Myth No. 4: The laws adopted in China are meaningless because the Chinese people file few lawsuits; Myth No. 5: Chinese statutes are intentionally vague and there is no guidance on interpretation from judges' commentary or case law (Dickinson, 2007). The fact that such "stale, old myths that can lead business people to make costly mistakes" (Dickinson, 2007) are still very much alive testifies to the sad state of the international community's understanding of the legal system of China.

Such misperceptions and unbalanced views, according to Peerenboom—the author of the 2002 book *China's Long March Toward Rule of Law* and the 2007 book *China Modernizes Threat to the West or Model for the Rest?* —are primarily attributable to the negative portrait of China's legal system by the Western media (2003). When they report on the legal system of China (and indeed China as a whole), Western journalists "tend to report the sensational" (Peerenboom, 2002: 561), often "to the exclusion of other important developments" (Peerenboom, 2002: 560), and they often "impose their own values" (Peerenboom,

2002: 560). Such approaches, according to Peerenboom, account for the "wide discrepancy between the remarkable progress that China has made in establishing a viable legal order and the exceedingly negative portraits of the legal system" (Peerenboom, 2002: 560). And given "the Western monopoly of global news services" (Khattak E. A., et al., 2012) and the resulting dominance of "Western viewpoints on world events" (Schenk S. & Ahmed M.), it is not surprising that the outside world's perception of China, including its legal system, should be negative and biased.

In view of this, it is necessary for China to step up its own efforts to introduce itself, including its legal system, to the rest of the world, in a fair and balanced way, so as to neutralize the adverse effect of the negative coverage by the western media, and thereby create a favorable international environment for its peaceful development. And given the fact that the Chinese language, though boasting of the largest number of native speakers and increasing influence in the world with the steady rise of its speaking population in recent years, is not widely used as a foreign language, such communication must be carried out in the languages of the target audience, especially English, the most widely used language in today's world and so far the dominant language in international communication (郭可, 2002). In the process, translation from Chinese into foreign languages, especially English, plays a vital role, according to some prominent Chinese scholars and veteran journalists and translators involved in presenting China to the world, and the quality of such translation directly determines the success or failure of the communication (爱泼斯坦，林戊荪，沈苏儒, 2000). Therefore, it is urgent to review the current practice and academic studies related to the translation aspect in the international communication of China's legal system, identify the problems that are holding back China's publicity efforts to introduce its legal system to the outside world and seek for solutions to such problems. This book is purported to be a tentative attempt in this regard.

1.2 Definitions

Before proceeding to discuss the practice and theory of the Chinese to English translation for the purpose of presenting China's legal system to the rest of the world, it is advisable to define some terms in the specific context of the book.

1.2.1 China

In the general context, the term "China" refers to the People's Republic of China, whose territory consists of the mainland of China (the Mainland), the Hong Kong Special Administrative Region (the Hong Kong SAR), the Macao Special Administrative Region (the Macao SAR) and the Taiwan region. However, as part of the legacy of foreign invasions and civil wars in the late 19th century and early 20th century, the aforementioned four parts of China are de facto separate jurisdictions, in spite of certain overlapping claims of jurisdiction. In view of this and for the purpose of the present book, when it is used in the expression "China's legal system", "the legal system of China" or any other expression of the same effect, the word "China" should be understood as referring to the mainland of China only. This interpretation, however, is strictly only used for academic purposes and should not be viewed as excluding the other three parts from the territory of China in any manner whatsoever.

1.2.2 International Communication

In the context of China and for the purpose of the present book, "international communication" refers to communication activities of China that aim at enhancing better understanding of China among vast overseas audiences as well as foreign nationals within the territory of China by presenting them with information from the perspective of China in a fair and balanced way. Such communication is conducted via media channels such as radio, TV, newspapers, news agencies and computer networks.

At present, the aforementioned activities may be designated by a number of terms in China, the most frequently used among which are "对外宣传 (*duiwai xuanchuan*, literally external propaganda)", "对外报道 (*duiwai baodao*, literally reporting to external audiences)", "对外传播 (*duiwai chuanbo*, or external communication)", "国际传播 (*guoji chuanbo*, or international communication)" and "全球传播 (*quanqiu chuanbo*, or global communication)". Among the five terms, the first one is the traditional term used in China to refer to its efforts to introduce itself to the rest of the world. However, there have been calls for the gradual phase-out of the term, because of the negative association of the literal English translation of the word, namely, "external propaganda" or "external publicity" (赵启正, 2009; 陆地, 高菲, 2005); in response to such calls and with the introduction of modern communication theories into China in recent decades, the latter four of the five terms have been recommended and promoted as more neutral alternatives of the term "对外宣传" ("外宣" for short). The four more favored terms, in spite of slight differences, refer to practically the same activities when they are used in the context of China' efforts to present itself to the international community, and therefore may be used as synonyms in the present book (unless where it is clearly indicated or purported otherwise). For example, in a news report by the Xinhua News Agency (the official news agency of China that plays an important role in China's international communication efforts) on the speech delivered by Li Changchun, the most senior government official in charge of China's international communication, on the 80th founding anniversary of the news agency, *Senior official urges Xinhua to improve global communication capacity*①, the term "global communication" and "international communication" are used synonymously as the English translation of "国际传播", "对外报道" and "对外传播" in the Chinese original of the speech② released by Xinhua.

However, it must be noted here that while the word "propaganda" is strongly derogatory in English, its literal equivalent "宣传" in Chinese is neutral and even positive on most occasions. Therefore, the term "对外宣传" and its short form "外宣" are still used side by side with its promoted replacements and prac-

---

① Retrieved from the website of the Xinhua News Agency at http://news.xinhuanet.com/english2010/china/2011-11/07/c_131233082.htm.

② 《李长春：在新华社建社 80 周年纪念大会上的讲话》(*Speech of Li Changchun Delivered at the Ceremony Marking the 80th Anniversary of the Xinhua News Agency*, translation by the author of the present book), retrieved from the website of the Xinhua News Agency at http://news.xinhuanet.com/politics/2011-11/09/c_122252816.htm.

tically interchangeable with them, in a "new wine in an old bottle" way, so to speak. For example, in a Xinhua report[①] carried by www. gov. cn, the official website of the Central Government of China, the Chinese terms "外宣", "国际传播", "对外报道" and "对外传播" are used synonymously to refer to the notion of "international communication". And in the context of the translation aspect of such communication, "外宣" remains dominant.

In recognition of the above situation, the traditional term "外宣", the short form of "对外宣传", is adopted as an umbrella term for all the above synonymous terms, for the purpose of convenience in the present book, without any negative association.

1.2.3 Translation for International Communication (外宣翻译)

The study of the translation for international communication, as suggested by its very name, is a cross-disciplinary undertaking that combines translation studies and the study of communication. It is relatively a new-comer in translation studies in China, and works in this field are few and far between, in comparison with those on the translation of literary works and even those on "applied translation", such as law, business, medicine, technology, etc.

The present book adopts the definition by Professor Zhang Jian, a prominent Chinese scholar in the field of theory and practice of international communication and translation—in the context of China, translation for international communication is a special form of translation. It is a communicative activity in which information in Chinese is presented to foreign audiences (including those within the territory of China) through various media in English (or any other foreign languages, as the case may be) for the purpose of facilitating the proper understanding of China by the rest of the world in the era of globalization. [外宣翻译是翻译的一种特殊形式，指在全球化背景下以让世界了解中国为目的，以汉语为信息源，以英语等外国语为信息载体，以各种媒体为渠道，以外国民众

① 《全国对外宣传工作会议1月4日至5日在北京召开》(*National Conference on International Communication Held Between Jan. 4 to 5*, translation by the author of the book) retrieved from the website of China's central government at http://www. gov. cn/jrzg/2011 -01/06/content _1779343. htm.

（包括境内的各类外籍人士）为对象的交际活动。][1]

It can be concluded from the above definition that：①Translation for the international communication of China (including its legal system, of course) is highly purposeful：It is oriented to and proceeds from presenting China to the intended audience (both in and outside China) in a balanced and truthful way so as to promote the understanding of China by the rest of the world, dispel the adverse effects of negative coverage of China by the western media and hence to improve the image of China. ②Translation is viewed as a communication process, instead of merely as a transformation on the linguistic level. ③Aside from the general rules of translation, translation for international communication is also subject to a number of specialized and unique rules. ④The essence of translation for international communication lies in the transfer of information, not merely the language forms. ⑤The scope of what is translated is very wide and practically covers all Chinese texts (both written and spoken), not just media texts. In this sense, translation for international communication cannot be equated with media translation or "applied translation" in a simplistic way.

1.2.4 Legal System

Definition of the term "legal system" varies. According to www.thedictionary.com, a website offering online dictionary functions, a legal system is "a system for interpreting and enforcing the laws", while the Cambridge Dictionaries Online, which claims itself to be the "most popular online dictionary and thesaurus for learners of English"[2], defines "legal system" rather differently as "the organizations and people in a country or area who work in the area of law". A third definition, by the prestigious English-Chinese Dictionary of Anglo-American Law, describes the legal system of a country as all the laws and regulations formulated in that country plus all the rules and norms according to which such laws and regulations are administered.

---

① 王仲贻，2011, translated by the author of the present book.

② http://dictionary.cambridge.org/, an online dictionary service provided by the Cambridge University Press.

For the present book and in the context of China, a broader definition of the term "legal system" is adopted, which combines some elements of the above three definitions—the legal system of China, for the purpose of the present book, refers to all forms of legislations of China (including the Constitution as well as all the laws formulated by the legislatures on all levels and governmental departments delegated by such legislatures), as well as the legislation (how laws are made), administration (how courts of law operate), enforcement (how laws are implemented) and academic study of laws.

1.2.5 Legal Texts

To the extent of the present book, legal texts are classified by the author into "hard legal texts" and "soft legal texts". In the former category are "traditional" legal texts, including laws, administrative regulations and other types of legislations, and other documents "which are, or may become, part of the judicial process, for instance, contracts, wills, court documents, witness statements and expert reports" (Harvey, 2002), as well as academic publications on law. Legal texts in this category may be further divided into prescriptive, descriptive and expressive legal texts and hybrid texts according to their functions. Such texts have been the subject of an extensive range of academic studies, including those on legal English (as a type of English for specific purposes), legal and judicial translation, etc.

In the latter category are other law-themed texts, such as media reports about legislations, specific civil, criminal or other types of legal cases, and law-themed literary works, which traditionally are not included as legal texts. Although such texts are unlikely to be part of the judicial process, they are primarily themed around law, be they the making, administrating, enforcement of law, and may provide valuable insights into the legal system of a country and therefore make excellent source texts in the translation for the international communication of China's legal system. For example, *The Celebrated Cases of Judge Dee* (*Digong An*), the English translation by Robert Van Gulik (高罗佩), a Dutch diplomat and prominent Sinologist, of a 18th century Chinese detective novel, not only introduced a genre in traditional Chinese literature, namely, the classic Chinese detective novels (公案小说) to the "western readers in general" for the first time (Gulik, 1976: Ⅱ – Ⅳ), but also played an important role in introducing the traditional Chinese legal system to the outside world, as is testified by the fact that this translation, which first came out in 1949, is still in print today①, both as an fascinating literary work and a must-read book for scholars from a variety of fields, including Asian studies, Chinese law, and Chinese history②.

1.2.6 Parallel Texts

Unlike in corpus linguistics, where parallel texts refer to "a corpus of translations, which is compared to the corresponding source texts, whereas a corpus of non-translated texts for comparison with translated texts is called 'comparable corpus'" (Nord, 2010), the present research adopts a more inclusive definition for the term "parallel texts": "Parallel texts are two linguistically independent products arising from an identical (or very similar) situation. They are used in translation studies and lexicography... for assessing how the same kind of factual material is verbalized in different languages... parallel texts are frequently used as aids in creating a natural and idiomatic translation... parallel texts often represent the 'model translation'." (Snell-Hornby, 2001: 86) Parallel texts are texts on comparable topics, which, despite being produced in differing environments, belong to the same genre and fulfill the same function. (House, 2007)

As a matter of fact, parallel texts are one of the three types of "auxiliary texts" described by Christiane Nord (2010), one of the leading figures of the German functionalist school of translation studies, which "may be of great help" (House, 2007) to translators: namely, previous translations (of the same or a

---

① According to the www.amazon.com, the world's leading online shopping website, this translation work by Gulik was reprinted as recently as in 2003 by Dover Publications Inc and made into an audio book by Blackstone Audiobooks in 2009.

② For example, *The Celebrated Cases of Judge Dee* (*Digong An*) is included on the syllabus of the course "Chinese Law and Society" of the University of California, Berkeley. Please refer to http://legalstudies.berkeley.edu/files/2012/02/LS161 – Law – in – Chinese – Society – Berring – Spring12 – syllabus.pdf.

similar text), which provide the translators with methodological information, background texts in which factual and linguistic or cultural information may be found, and parallel texts, which provide information on genre and style conventions but also on forms of expression, collocations, idiomatic language use, register, and so on. Nord defines parallel texts as target-culture texts of the same or a similar type as the source-culture texts. Sometimes, "a parallel text is so much like a translation of the source text in question that it can serve as a model for the translation" (House, 2007). In this case, such parallel texts may be used as model texts by translators.

To sum up, in the present book a parallel text of a source text refers to such as target-culture text as is of similar or the same genre as the source text, and fulfills the same function.

So far, six important terms have been defined to avoid misunderstanding and lay the foundation for further discussion of the Chinese to English translation of soft legal texts in the context of China's international communication to present its legal system to the rest of the world. In the next section, academic studies related to this emerging field will be reviewed to provide important inspirations for the following chapters of the book.

1.3 Research Questions of the Present Book

The present book sets out to find answers to the following questions:

(1) What is the current state of Chinese to English translation for the international communication of China's legal system like?

(2) What kinds of problems are such translation faced with?

(3) What possible solutions are there to such problems?

(4) What implications does the present book have for the fields of study related to the present book?

1.4 Theoretical Framework and Methodology of the Present Book

The theoretical framework of the present book comprises two parts, namely, the rules and principles formed by veteran translators, journalists, editors and administrators engaged in the translation for China's international communication on the basis of their experiences and expertise and the German functionalist approach to translation studies, especially the Skopos Theory.

1.4.1 Rules and Principles Drawn Up by Veteran Journalists and Translators

During the 60-odd years since the founding of the People's Republic of China in 1949, China's international communication practitioners, including translators, journalists, editors and administrators, have formulated a number of rules and principles on the Chinese to English translation involved in China's efforts to introduce herself to the rest of the world on the basis of their accumulated experiences and professional expertise.

The most prominent among such rules and principles include "Three In-line-with principles" and "interpretive translation".

1.4.1.1 "Three In-line-with Principles" of China's International Communication (外宣"三贴近"原则)

In accordance with "Three In-line-with Principles", China's international communication efforts must be in line with the actual state of development of China, the content of such efforts must be in line with the targeted audience's need for information on China and the translated texts used for China's international communication must be in line with the norms and conventions in the culture of such targeted language (English, in the context of the present book) to ensure that such external publicity efforts of China will achieve their intended effect, namely, providing the audiences with true and balanced information on

China and create a favorable international environment for China's development (黄友义, 1999).

1.4.1.2 The Rule of "Interpretive Translation"

In the context of China's international communication efforts, the rule of "interpretive translation" was first proposed by Duan Liancheng (段连城), who, based on decades of experiences as a translator and from the perspective of cross-cultural communication, argued that when translating general external publicity materials (materials other than official documents), the translator should be allowed to process the Chinese original of such materials (段连城, 2004: 176).

The processing tactics include adding background information necessary for the intended readers to fully understand such translations, avoiding literal translation of clichés and grandiose and empty parts of such parts but rendering the information behind them in a language style appropriate in the target text readers' culture, and rearranging the layout of the texts, i. e., the order of sentences and even paragraphs, in light of the norms and conventions in the target readers' culture (段连城, 2004: 177).

1.4.2 The German Functionalist Approach to Translation Study

In the present book, the German functionalism, the German functional approach (to translation studies) and the German functionalist school of translation studies are used interchangeably as synonyms where the context permits, referring to a function-based approach to translation studies formed by a number of German scholars in the 1970s. According to Christiane Nord, a prominent figure of the German functionalist school of translation studies, functionalism is an approach "where the translator's decisions are governed by the intended function of the target text or any of its parts" (2001: 138). Important features of German functionalism include:

1.4.2.1 Translational Action

Based on the action theory, the German functionalism adopts a new term "translation action" as a "generic term... designed to cover all forms of intercultural transfer, including those which do not involve any source or target texts" (Nord, 2001a: 141). Translational action is broader than the term "translation" in the traditional sense: "Translational action" refers the range of what translators actually do; on the other hand, "translation" refers to what translators do when they are rendering texts (Nord, 2001a: 17).

Within the framework of German functionalism, translation is defined as an intentional, interpersonal, partly verbal intercultural interaction. Notably, in the model of translational action, the translation process involves six figures, in addition to the source text producer, translator, and target text receiver present in other approaches to translation studies, three more participants are introduced: the client, who is the translation initiator [who is the party "who actually needs the target text" (Nord, 2001a: 20)], the translation commissioner [the party that "asks the translator to produce a target text for a particular purpose and addressee" (Nord, 2001a: 20).] and the final user of the target text. The role of the initiator is very important in that it is the initiator that decides the translation purpose. However, since the initiator, who in many cases is not expert on cross-cultural communication, is either unwilling or unable to specify the translation purpose (Nord, 2001a: 30), the translator, with his or her competence and expertise, may negotiate with the initiator over the translation purpose and may even advise the initiator not to communicate in the intended way. In this way, the translator in the German functional approach has a greater say in the translation process, with his or her elevated to the status of "responsible expert" (Nord, 2001a: 30).

1.4.2.2 The Skopos Theory

"Skopos" is a Greek word meaning "purpose". According to the Skopos Theory (German: Skopostheorie), the "prime principle determining any translation process is the purpose (Skopos) of the overall translational action" (Nord, 2001a: 140). This theory provides three rules for translation, namely the Skopos Rule, the Coherence Rule and the Fidelity rule.

The Skopos Rule is the top-ranking rule for any translation, which says that a translational action is determined by its Skopos; that is, "the end justifies the means" (Nord, 2001a: 29).

The Coherence Rule means that what the translator can and should do is to produce a target text that is at least likely to be meaningful to the target-text receivers.

According to the Fidelity Rule, the target language text and source language text (which are viewed as two offers of information) should bear some kind of relationship (Nord, 2001a: 32).

Note that the term "some kind of relationship" is used in the Fidelity Rule, instead of "equivalence" or "faithfulness" used in other translation research approaches. Behind this conspicuous phenomenon is an important feature of German functionalism: adequacy, instead of equivalence, as the translation quality assessment standard.

1.4.2.3 Adequacy

In German functionalism, adequacy is adopted as the standard for assessing translation quality. A translation is deemed as adequate as long as it fulfills the requirements of the translation brief (Nord, 2001a: 35), an important concept in the functionalist approach that prescribes the communicative purpose of the translation and provides the translator with information on the intended target-text function(s), the target-text addressee(s), the medium(s) over which it will be transmitted, the time and place and the motive for production and reception of the target text (Nord, 2001a: 137).

In German functionalism, adequacy is a superordinate term of equivalence. In other words, equivalence is a form of adequacy. It is necessary and desirable only when the translation brief requires it (Nord, 2001a: 35).

1.4.2.4 Classification of Translation Strategies and Translation Problems

Based on the intended function of the target text, translation may be divided into documentary translation and instrumental translation, and the two forms of translation may be further divided into sub-types. The two types of translations will be defined and analyzed in chapter four of the present book.

Furthermore, the German functionalist approach also classifies translation problems (which are objective and will remain whether they are solved or not) into four types, namely pragmatic translation problems, cultural translation problems, linguistic translation problems and text-specific translation problems. The failures in solving such translation problems, i. e., translation errors, are then classified correspondingly into four types, pragmatic, cultural, linguistic and text-specific. On the basis of these classifications, the German functionalist school advocates a "top-down" approach to translation problems, such problems are to be dealt with in the order of pragmatic problems, cultural problems, linguistic problems and text-specific problems.

1.4.2.5 The Role of Auxiliary Texts in Achieving Translation Adequacy

As has been defined in Section 1. 2. 6 of the present book, "auxiliary texts" are divided into three types, namely, previous translations, background texts, and parallel texts. Among them, previous translations (of the same or a similar text) provide the translators with methodological information; background texts offer factual and linguistic or cultural information; and parallel texts provide the translators with information on the genre and style conventions as well as forms of expression, collocations, idiomatic language use, register, and so on.

Auxiliary texts play an important role in helping the translators achieve adequacy in the Chinese to English translation for China's international communication, because such translation, judged by the rules and principles drawn up by veteran Chinese international communication practitioners, is overwhelmingly instrumental translation in that the target texts must conform to the conventions and norms of the target culture, not those of the source culture.

1.4.2.6 Summary

Since it was first introduced into China more than two decades ago in 1987, German functionalism has been applied in a number of areas in translation study in China, including translation criticism, translation strategies, and those for literary translation and non-literary translation, and translation training (卞建

华，崔永禄，2006）. Notably, as will be discussed in detail in the subsequent two chapters, this approach to translation studies has been applied to the translation for China's international communication efforts, because this approach, with its emphasis on the translation purpose, allowance of receiver-centeredness, greater flexibility and higher status for the translator, echoes with the rules and principles formulated by Chinese translators and journalists and provides systematic theory support to the study of the Chinese to English translation for China's efforts to present itself to the rest of the world. That is why the German functionalism is chosen as the bedrock of the theoretical framework of this study, which will be discussed in detail in Chapter Three of this book.

1.4.3 Scope and Methodology of the Present Research

As will be demonstrated in Chapter Two and Chapter Three, the current academic studies on and practice of the Chinese to English translation of soft legal texts in the context of international communication of China's legal system are focused on hard legal texts, such as legislative texts and other legal documents that are involved and may potentially be involved in legal proceedings, such as official documents of judicial organs and contracts and agreements. Such texts, important as they are for a proper understanding of China's legal system, are rather elitist and technical in nature, and therefore are mostly intended for legal professionals and parties involved in legal proceedings (who, more often than not, have to rely on the services of legal professionals anyway). Such over-dependence on hard legal texts inevitably limits the coverage of China's efforts in this regard and is detrimental to achieving the intended goal of such efforts, namely, introducing the legal system of China to the general public, i. e., the laypeople as well as legal professionals, as may be inferred from the definition of both "international communication" and "translation for international communication". On the other hand, the vast quantities of soft legal texts, such as law-themed media reports which are oriented to a far more inclusive readership, are left out of the academic picture. In view of this, the present research, as the first of its kind, takes the translation of such soft legal texts as its subject and attempts to provide solutions to problems in such translation after an overall review thereof.

The present book is based on a case-based empirical study, in which concrete examples of translations of soft legal texts will be examined to identify the problems therein and propose solutions for such problems within the framework of German functionalism as well as the rules and principles formulated by veteran translators, journalists and administrators involved in China's international communication.

1.5 Originalities of the Present Book

The present research is original in the following aspects:

(1) It expands the scope of the concept "legal texts" by including "soft legal texts", especially the law-themed media reports.

(2) It is the first academic study to systematically review the current state of the Chinese to English translation of soft legal texts in the context of international communication of China's legal system (中国法律外宣汉英翻译).

(3) It analyzes the problems in the Chinese to English translation of soft legal texts and proposes solutions thereto within the framework of German functionalism and on the basis of the rules and principles formed on the experiences and expertise of practitioners engaged in the international communication of China.

(4) It confirms the viability of German functionalism as theoretical guidelines for China's international communication efforts on the basis of a proper examination of its relation with the rules and principles mentioned in the previous paragraphs.

1.6 Structure of the Present Book

The present book consists of seven chapters.

Chapter One introduces the background of the present research and lays the foundation for the present book by defining a number of crucial terms and expressions, identifying the research questions, theoretical framework, scope, methodology and originalities of the present research and describing the structure of this book. It highlights the embarrassing fact that there is a serious imbalance between the demand for and supply of genuine and comprehensive information about the legal system in China because of the misrepresentation by the dominant Western media and the ineffectiveness of China's efforts to present its legal system to the rest of the world. To meet the need for information on China's legal system, which is increasingly relevant to many people in the world given the gradual rise of China and the ongoing globalization process, and to dispel the misperception of China's legal system and thereby create a favorable international environment for China's development, it is therefore necessary to improve China's international communication efforts related to its legal system and hence the significance and timelines of the present research.

Chapter Two is an overview of China's efforts to introduce its legal system to the rest of the world. A historical review is first made about the Chinese to English translation related to the legal system of China from the early 1800s to the mid-20th century. Then this chapter goes on to focus on the translation for introducing China's legal system to the outside world in the modern era, which is reviewed from a number of angles and the quality (or rather lack of quality) of such translation is highlighted with a translated text sample selected from one of the websites of the top judicial organs of China. Finally, a conclusion on the current state of the translation practice is made based on such analysis—the translation and release of hard legal texts are dominant while that of soft legal texts are marginalized, although the latter may reach a much wider audience.

In Chapter Three, a comprehensive review of publications concerning the theme of the present research is conducted. It is found that although "legal translation" and "translation for international communication", two fields related to the present study are receiving increasing academic attention, there is yet to be an academic attempt at the issue of the translation of soft legal texts. Findings of the existing publications on the two aforementioned topics are then summarized on the basis of a thorough review to serve as reference and inspiration for the present research. Finally, on the basis of the findings of the previous two chapters, it is proposed that a systematic study be made to analyze the translation problems related to the translation of soft legal texts.

Chapter Four of the present book specifies the theoretical foundation and guidance for the study proposed in the previous chapters. It examines the German functionalist approach to translation and its applicability and relevance to the present research. The main concepts, principles, rules and ideas of German functionalism are introduced and analyzed. Then a comparison is made between the German functionalism and the rules and principles proposed by long-time practitioners of China's international publicity on the basis of their experiences and expertise, confirming that the two are in line with each other and therefore the former may be used as theoretical guideline for the Chinese to English translation of soft legal texts in the context of international communication of China's legal system.

In Chapter Five, the Chinese to English translation of soft legal texts in the context of international communication of China's legal system is examined within the framework of German functionalism and the translation strategies, problems and solutions are proposed. After an analysis of the Skopos of the Chinese to English translation for the purpose of introducing China's legal system and the intended functions of the target texts produced through such translation, it is concluded that such translation should be instrumental translation under the German functional model. Accordingly, a top-down functionalist approach to translation problem-solving is proposed as the strategy guiding China's efforts to introduce its legal system through Chinese to English translation. This chapter then goes on to introduce the important role played by auxiliary texts in helping the translators implement the translation strategy, identify and solve translation problems.

In Chapter Six, translation errors are selected from soft legal texts released by both specialized and concurrent international communication entities of China, and are examined according to the German functionalist approach to identify the cause of such errors and propose solutions thereto.

Chapter Seven is the conclusion of the present study, in which the findings in the previous five chapters are consolidated, and implications of the present study to related fields and limitations of the present research are listed as suggestions for further research.

Chapter Two Chinese to English Translation in the Context of International Communication of China's Legal System: An Overview

In the present chapter, the current practice of the Chinese to English translation for China's international communication of its legal system will be reviewed to identify the problems therein.

2.1 A Historical Review

It is no exaggeration to say that the Chinese to English translation of China's legal system has played a crucial role in the relationship between China and the English-speaking world. As a matter of fact, the first ever complete Chinese work (and the first ever Chinese statute, for that matter) to be directly translated from Chinese into English is none other than *Law Code of the Great Qing Dynasty* (《大清律例》), a system of fundamental laws of feudal China and explanatory notes considered as "the central element... of the formal legal system of the Chinese Empire" (Jones, 1994: I). This seminal and unprecedented translation enterprise by Sir George Thomas Staunton (1781 – 1859), which was published under the title "*Ta Tsing Leu Lee: Being the Fundamental Laws, and a Selection from the Supplementary Statute of the Penal Code of China*" (for convenience of identification, hereinafter referred uniformly as *Law Code of the Great Qing Dynasty*) came at a time of rapid expansion of trade between the Qing Dynasty of China and the British Empire in the era of industrial revolution, and was "part and parcel of the larger intellectual enterprise to decipher and domesticate the 'inscrutable' 'China' / 'Orient', which had become imperative for the further expansion of Western Capitalism, Christianity, and colonies in the Asia-Pacific" (Li, 2007: 1). This translated version was to remain "the only English translation of the imperial Chinese law code for over one and a half centuries"

(Li, 2007: 2).

The laws of the Republic of China, which was founded after the 1911 Chinese Revolution that ended the Qing Dynasty and the feudal rule of more than two millennia in China, were also translated into English, as was testified by the translation of the *Civil Code of the Republic of China* (Ching-lin Hsia, James L. E. Chow, Liu Chieh and Yukon Chang, 1931).

However, due to the limitation of space, the book primarily focuses on the Chinese to English translation of the legal system of China in the modern era, i. e., after the founding of the People's Republic of China in 1949, especially since the late 1970s when China started to implement the policy of reform and opening-up.

2.2 Chinese to English Translation in the International Communication of China's Legal System in the Modern Era

Since its founding in 1949, the People's Republic of China has always attached importance to introducing its legal system to the rest after the world through English, the lingua franca of the world. Within weeks after the birth of the People's Republic, *The Common Program of the Chinese People's Political Consultative Conference* (hereinafter, referred to as the CPPCC) and *the Organic Law of the Central People's Government of the People's Republic of China*, two fundamental legal documents that served as the provisional constitution of China before the enactment of the Constitution in 1954 (Houn, 1955), along with other documents adopted by the CPPCC (which was the de facto national parliament of the People's Republic of China before the National People's Congress was elected and convened in 1954) were translated into English and published by the Foreign Languages Press of China, a publisher deeply involved in the international communication in China.

Along with the development of the People's Republic of China, a number of other important laws, including *Marriage Law of the People's Republic of China* (an enactment that enshrines gender equality and prohibits arranged marriages) and *Agrarian Reform Law of the People's Republic of China* (which effectively ends the feudal land ownership system on the mainland of China that had lasted for more than two thousand years) were also translated into English and published soon after their enactment and promulgation, and the revised and updated versions of such translated laws were also re-published in later years.

Since the late 1970s and for the purpose of advancing its modernization drive, China has been striving to restore its legal system that had been greatly damaged during the chaos of the Cultural Revolution and promote the rule of law, with a large number of laws and administrative regulations formulated and promulgated along the way. In this way, its legal system has been gradually restored and improved. In addition, in response to the rapidly increase in exchanges with the rest of the world, China has stepped up its international communicative efforts to introduce its legal system to the rest of the world, aiming at "facilitating economic development and the reform and opening-up of China" (王明新, 2009) by "cultivating a positive image of China and creating a conducive international environment for China" (王明新, 2009). In comparison with its first three decades of the new country, a much greater part of China's fundamental laws and administrative regulations have been translated into English in the 30-odd years after 1978, as is testified by the ongoing systematic translation and publication of China's legislations, such as *Laws of the People's Republic of China* by the Foreign Languages Press which are English editions of Chinese laws and regulations chronologically (from 1979 to 1996) and selectively compiled and translated by the Legislative Affairs Commission of the Standing Committee of the National People's Congress of the People's Republic of China, the Chinese and English bilingual series by Law Press China and China Legal System Publishing House, and the more recent translation work overseen by the Legislative Affairs Office of the State Council as part of China's commitment to the World Trade Organization. In addition to individual laws, a number of documents that provide a panoramic view on the entire Chinese legal system or specific sections thereof have also been translated and released, such as the 1991 government white paper *Human Rights in China*[①], the 1992 government white paper on the criminal jus-

① Retrieved from http://www.china.org.cn/e-white/7/index.htm.

tice of China, *Criminal Reform in China*①, *the 2008 government white paper systematically reviewing the progress in the rule of law in China*, *China's Efforts and Achievements in Promoting the Rule of Law*②, and the most comprehensive government document so far on the legal system of China, *The Socialist System of Laws with Chinese Characteristics*③ published in November 2011. Notably, a number of translated works that aim at introducing China's legal system from a more reader-friendly perspective have also appeared. For example, a number of books and pamphlets about China's legal system targeting "the laypeople", i. e., those who are not legal professionals, have come out, such as *The Law and Lore of the Chinese Criminal Justice* by Sydney Shapiro, a naturalized Chinese citizen who was a practicing lawyer before coming to China and has been one of the most prominent individuals engaged in China's external publicity efforts.

In the 21st century, with the steady rise of China and its closer integration into the international community, as manifested by its accession to the World Trade Organization and its "increasingly assertive and proactive stance" (Olson and Prestowitz, 2011) "within a variety of international organizations" (Olson and Prestowitz, 2011), and boosted by the development of new technologies, notably the computer and the Internet, China's international communicative efforts to introduce its legal system have undergone further expansion and diversification. In the following part of this section, the present-day Chinese to English translation for the purpose of the international communication of China's legal system will be introduced from different perspectives.

2. 2. 1 Classification in Terms of Translation Initiator

In terms of the translation initiator, one of the six participants of the translation process in the German functionalist approach, who is the client (a person, group or institution) initiating the translation process, Chinese to English translation of soft legal texts in the context of international communication of China's

---

① Retrieved from http://www.china.org.cn/e-white/criminal/index.htm.

② Retrieved from http://www.china.org.cn/government/news/2008-02/28/content_11025486.htm.

③ Retrieved from http://www.gov.cn/english/2011-10/27/content_1979838.htm.

legal system may be divided two categories, namely, translation initiated by an initiator on the stance of China, which aims at "exporting" information on the legal system of China to the outside world, and in the second category translation initiated by clients on the stance of a foreign country, international organization, institution or individual, which, in contrast, aims at "importing" information on the Chinese legal system into that country or for the benefit of that international organization, institution or individual. For the purpose of the book, only translation in the first category, i. e. , those sponsored by a China-based organization, whether a governmental agency or non-government institution, is deemed as translation for the international communication of China's legal system (中国法律外宣), while translation in the second category may be used as valuable reference for translation practitioners and the products may provide important insights as "auxiliary texts" as defined by Nord.

2.2.2 Classification in Terms of Translator

Generally, English translations for the purpose of introducing China's legal system, like the overall international communication efforts of China, may be classified into three categories according to the identity of the translators, namely: ①translations carried out exclusively by "foreign experts", native-users of the English language; ②those that come out as the fruits of the joint efforts of Chinese translators and "foreign experts", who serve as revisers and editors of the translations of their Chinese partners; and ③ those exclusively done by Chinese translators who are not native users of the English language. In actual translation practice, the latter two models still remain dominant, although they are against the generally accepted norms of translation services, which require the translator to translate from foreign languages into his or her mother tongue. This state of affairs is primarily attributable to the fact that the number of native-users of the English language who have sufficient proficiency of the Chinese language is rather limited and therefore, the Chinese to English translation of the international publicity materials of China—those on the Chinese legal system included—has to rely on Chinese translators (黄友义, 2011). As a result, the quality of the translation products based on the latter two models varies and sometimes actually negatively affects the effectiveness of the international communication that such translation is purported to serve (爱泼斯坦，林戊荪，沈苏儒，2000). Since it takes time and money to train a sufficient contingent of Chinese to English translators consisting of native users of the English language, the latter two of the three existing models is expected to remain dominant, and in view of this, some veteran translators and journalists engaged in China's international publicity have been calling for greater attention to improving translation quality by enhancing the training of Chinese translators and employing the service of more "foreign experts" (爱泼斯坦，林戊荪，沈苏儒，2000).

2.2.3 Classification in Terms of Transmission Medium

In terms of the medium or media through which they are released, Chinese to English translation for the purpose of presenting China's legal system to the outside world may be divided into two categories, namely, those released through "traditional" specialized international communication organs of China, and those released via newer and concurrent media.

In the first category are the translations released through organizations that are traditionally associated with China's international communication efforts, including the foreign department of news agencies (such as the Xinhua News Agency, the national news agency of China that is playing an increasingly influential role in the world), print publications (including law-themed books, pamphlets, as those mentioned in Section 4.2 of the present book); foreign language newspapers and magazines, such as *Beijing Review* (formerly titled *Peking Review*, the leading foreign language news weekly of China), *China Today* (formerly titled *China Reconstructs*, which is the "only multi-language and general-interest monthly in China"①), *China Daily* (the first national English-language daily newspaper on the mainland of China), *China Pictorial* (a general-interest illustrated magazine), and a number of regional English language newspapers and

① http://www.chinatoday.com.cn/English/20021/voice1.htm.

magazines; the English service of radio and television networks, including China Radio International (formerly known as Radio Peking and Radio Beijing, the leading international radio broadcaster of China's mainland), the English Channel of China Central Television (the CCTV, China's national television broadcaster) and some regional television stations of China.

Notably, with the advent of the information age, a number of multilingual websites have been launched in China for the purpose of introducing China to the rest of the world. Such websites may be further divided into "general-interest" websites that aim at giving the users a panoramic view of China and those specialize in introducing the legal system of China. Websites of the former type include www.china.gov, the official web portal of China's central government, and www.china.org.cn, which is "an authorized government portal site... under the auspices of the State Council Information Office and the China International Publishing Group (CIPG) in Beijing"①, and aims at providing "broad access to up-to-date news about China, with searchable texts of government papers and a wealth of basic information about Chinese history, politics, economics and culture"②, and www.english.peopledaily.com.cn, the English version of the website of *People's Daily*, the official newspaper of the ruling Communist Party of China.

Websites falling into the second category are those specially dedicated to introducing the legal system of China, or specific aspects thereof, such as www.npc.com.cn, the official website of the National People's Congress, China's top legislature, and http://www.chinalaw.gov.cn/, the official website of the Legislative Affairs Office of the State Council, both of which specialize in providing visitors with information on the legislative aspect of China's legal system); www.fdi.com.cn, a web portal operated under the auspice of the Ministry of Commerce of the Chinese government that aims at promoting foreign direct investment (FDI) in China and offers information on China's legal system, especially legal and judicial information related to investment, and www.lawinfochina.com, which is established and operated by Peking University, one of the

---

① http://www.china.org.cn/2009-09/28/content_18620394.htm.

② http://www.china.org.cn/2009-09/28/content_18620394.htm.

most prestigious institutions of higher education on the Mainland of China, and the Legal Information Center of the university. This website "strives to provide users with the most comprehensive and user-friendly services for online Chinese legal research. Currently, we supply a suite of bilingual (Chinese to English) databases complementing our more comprehensive Chinese-language offerings[①]". This website is by far the most comprehensive in China in terms of legal information provided in English. However, it must be noted that unless other websites, most of the services of the website are offered on a paid basis.

It should be made clear here that the classification in this category is not absolute. The same translation may be released by more than one form of media. With the wide application of information technology, almost all the leading "traditional" international communication organs have "gone online" by launching their own official websites, which usually provide more multi-media information. Take *Beijing Review* for example, the translation of a Chinese law, which is deemed as "official" and "formal" by the Chinese government, is available both in the print version and online with electronic version of the magazine. And the full text of the 2011 government white paper *The Socialist System of Laws with Chinese Characteristics* was actually released by the print media (*Beijing Review* and *China Daily*), the websites of these two print media and the web portal www. china. org. cn.

In addition to the above institutions traditionally associated with the international communication of China's legal system, some other players may also be included as an important force in promoting China in the context of the present book. Although they are not the first to be associated with the international publicity efforts of China, international communication agencies in this category may also play a positive role in presenting China's legal system. They include: the English versions of websites of central government ministries, local government departments, government-sponsored institutions, publications—both in print and electronic—by such non-governmental bodies as academic institutions, business and industry associations.

---

① Retrieved from http://www. lawinfochina. com/ProductsServices/index. shtm#aboutus.

The institutions in this category are not traditionally viewed as external publicity agencies of China, either because they are relative newcomers (such as the aforementioned English websites, which only came into existence after the wide application of information technology) in comparison with the well-recognized institutions like the Xinhua News Agency (first founded in 1931) and *Beijing Review* (founded in 1958), or because their intended purposes are facilitating the work of their owners (such as the English versions of government agencies), promoting academic exchange (in the case of academic institutions) or encouraging the development of business and industry (in the case of the print and electronic publication by industry associations). However, according to the definition adopted in the book, as long as information on China's legal system is rendered into English and released via them, such institutions may be viewed as legitimate international communication institutions, albeit they are concurrent ones (as against exclusive or specialized ones).

For example, the English version of the official website of the Ministry of Agriculture (MOA) of China, a governmental body that is not often associated with China's international communication efforts, includes a special section dedicated to "policies, laws and regulations"①, which are primarily English translations of government policies and legislations on or related to agriculture, which English-readers can access and copy for free. In addition, the section of "MOA Bulletin" presents English versions of the announcements, orders and decrees of the Ministry (which have the status of by-laws in China) promulgated in recent years.

Another case in point is www. sipo. gov. cn, which is the official website of the State Intellectual Property Office (SIPO), a government agency created to address domestic and international intellectual property issues. The English version of the website, which is purported to provide patent and other intellectual-property-related information to the visitors, provides English translations of a range of government policies and legislations, as well as by-laws formulated by the SIPO under the section "policy and law (sic)".

---

① Retrieved from official website of the Ministry of Agriculture of the People's Republic of China at http://english. agri. gov. cn/ga/plar/.

Of course, this typology of translations from the perspective of the media used may also be based on the technical nature of such media: whether they are print media, such as books, newspapers and magazines, etc., or electronic media, such as television, radio and computer network.

2.2.4 Classification in Terms of Text Receiver

From the perspective of the target text receiver, Chinese to English translation of soft legal texts in the context of international communication of China's legal system may be divided into two categories, namely translations of hard legal texts and those of soft legal texts (as defined in section 1.2.5 of the present book). The former, which are translations of legislative texts, legal documents and academic literature, are highly technical, professional and therefore elitist in nature, and are hence primarily intended for legal professionals, scholars and parties involved in legal proceedings (who, often than not, would rely on the services of lawyers with regard to such texts); translations in the second category, namely translations of soft legal texts, such as law-themed media reports, are far less technical and professional in nature and therefore are more "reader-friendly", serving both the legal professionals and scholars as well as the laypeople (the latter, it is reasonable to believe, far outnumber the former even in over-lawyered societies like the United States).

In spite of its far more inclusive readership, soft legal texts nonetheless takes a back seat to hard legal texts in translation related to the foreign publicity efforts of China, as may be testified by the following facts—while there are a number of institutions specializing in releasing translations of hard legal texts, such as laws, administrative regulations, departmental by-laws and/or law-themed academic publications such as www.lawinfochina.com, http://www.chinalaw.gov.cn, and the magazine *China Law* (《中国法律》, an bilingual academic journal sponsored by the Ministry of Justice of the People's Republic of China and published in Hong Kong), and many more international communication institutions of China have set aside special sections to release translations of hard legal texts, such as the above mentioned government bodies (ministries and commissions of the central government and departments and bureaus of local governments), legislatures (the website of the National People's Congress, and local legislatures), judicial organs (such as http://en.chinacourt.org/, the English version of the official website of the Supreme People's Court, China's highest court of law) and law enforcement organs (such as the Ministry of Public Security and local police departments).

On the other hand, however, there is yet to be a Chinese international communication body specifically dedicated to releasing translations of soft legal texts. Notably, none of the leading entities engaged in the international communication of China, such as *China Daily*, *Beijing Review*, the English Channel of China Central Television, including their websites, has a law column or section at all [with the exception, however, of China Radio International, whose feature program *Frontline* ("社会前沿"), a 25-minute documentary-like weekly radio program, which intends to help the listeners to "know more about China's legal framework and its effects on a rapidly changing society"① by presenting legal cases involving "compelling real-life stories"②]. So far, only three international communication institutions of China have bothered to set aside a section at all for releasing English translations of some kinds of soft legal texts, such as "judicial news" (as in the case of www.legalinfo.gov.cn/english/News1/node_7604.htm, which is the English version of the website of the Ministry of Justice and that of the Supreme People's Court, http://en.chinacourt.org/), or "legal news" (as in the case of www.lawinfochina.com). In addition, the former two of the three institutions are poorly maintained, with the contents of their releases seldom updated and the quality of the translation being substandard in many cases, as will be shown in the following section of the present chapter; while the third (www.lawinfochina.com), though regularly updated, primarily relies on news reports released by Chinese and overseas news agencies and media outlets, such as Xinhua, Reuters, and *China Daily*, and therefore are rather limited in cov-

---

① See the profile of the program on the official website of China Radio International at http://english.cri.cn/8706/2010/01/30/179s546654.htm.

② See the profile of the program on the official website of China Radio International at http://english.cri.cn/8706/2010/01/30/179s546654.htm.

erage. Though the website also provides more customized translations of soft legal texts, such as typical cases, legislative updates, etc, such contents are available to paying members only and hence are limited in readership. Other translations of soft legal texts are released under headings such as "business" (as in the case of *China Daily*) or "China" (as the case of China Central Television website) or simply as part of news in general. As a result, translations of soft legal texts are rather scattered in distribution and therefore it would be difficult for potential receivers to just locate such translated texts, let alone getting a proper understanding of China's legal system by reading such texts.

By contrast, many leading news media in the English-speaking world have their respective features or sections specializing in law-themed reports, which are either simply titled as "law" (as in the case of the British newspaper *The Guardian*, at http://www.guardian.co.uk/law) "legal news" (as in the case of CNN, at http://edition.cnn.com/JUSTICE/index.html), or "law news" (as in the case of Bloomberg, at http://www.bloomberg.com/news/law/), and all the law-related reports and other texts may be accessed to and copied for free. In particular, there are even websites specifically dedicated to following the dynamics of China's legal system, such as the "www.chinalawdigest.com".

2.3 Summary of This Chapter

So far, the translation of legal texts for the international communication of China has been reviewed from different perspectives, namely, the initiator, the translator, the medium used and the addressees. From this review, the following conclusions may be drawn:

First, with China's determination and efforts to restore and promote the rule of law, Chinese to English translation for the external publicity of China's legal system has been receiving increasing attention since the late 1970s, as is testified by the rapid increase in the amount of legal texts translated and released, and the increase and diversification of initiators.

Second, the media through which the translated legal texts are released for the purpose of introducing China's legal system to the outside world have increased and diversified. With the advent of the information technology, translated legal texts are now released either through websites specializing in such international communication or on a concurrent basis. In addition, traditional international communication institutions of China have also diversified into the cyber space to make their services more readily accessible to the addressees.

Third, translations of hard legal texts are released through far more media and in a more concentrated manner than translations of soft legal texts. As in the academic studies on the Chinese to English translation for introducing China's legal system to the rest of the world, the translations of hard legal texts are receiving far greater attention than that of soft legal texts, although the latter, being less technical and professional in nature, are more accessible to more receivers.

Fourth, under the current model of Chinese to English translation of soft legal texts in the context of international communication of China's legal system, there exists a remarkable disparity between the addressees and receivers of the translated texts. Addressees are different from receivers in that the former are the prospective receivers seen from the text producer's standpoint, in other words, they are the receivers that the text producer has in mind when producing the text, while the receivers, on the other hand, refer to those who actually read, listen to or otherwise process the text after they are produced. Since the international communication of China is intended for overseas addressees who are "people from all walks of life" (张昆, 2005), i. e., the well-educated elites and people with average education and economic means, it is reasonable to assume that the Chinese to English translation for China's efforts to introduce its legal system to the rest of the world should also serve a balanced mix of audiences, especially when such efforts are directed at "countries and regions where public opinions plays a crucial role" (张昆, 2005). In light of this, the current translation practice cannot fully achieve its intended purpose, i. e., to provide balanced information on China's legal system and thereby contribute to creating a favorable international environment for China, since the majority of resources are devoted to the translation and release of hard legal texts, which by their very nature, primarily serve the elite legal professionals in the target culture, instead of the typical average addressee who has a high school education and knows very little about

China (黎信, 2009: 22), including its legal system.

Above are a panoramic view of the practice of Chinese to English translation of soft legal texts in the context of international communication of China's legal system. In the following section, we will have a closer look at such translation practice, which, as has been pointed out by veteran external publicity practitioners of China, plays a crucial role in ensuring the effectiveness of China international communication efforts (爱泼斯坦, 林戊荪, 沈苏儒, 2000).

Chapter Three Literature Review

As has been pointed out in the first chapter of the present book, with the peaceful rise of China and the ongoing globalization process, there has been an increasingly urgent demand for knowledge about China, including its legal system, and on the other hand, China has become keenly aware of the need to introduce itself to the international community so as to create a favorable environment for its development. And with China's efforts in this regard in full swing and the prevailingly negative perception of China's legal system and the conspicuous lack of understanding of China's legal system, it is reasonable to assume that the study of how to present China's legal system to the rest of the world would receive its fair share of academic attention. However, as far as the data available to the author is concerned, there is yet to be an academic attempt to study the Chinese to English translation of China's legal system from the perspective of international communication; this topic still remains a virgin land, so to speak. This glaring absence of academic attempts in this regard is the very trigger of the present research.

However, as its name suggests, Chinese to English translation for the purpose of introducing China's legal system to the rest of the world, is closely associated with two other fields of study, namely, legal translation (法律翻译) and translation for international communication. In blazing trails in the brand-new academic effort, studies on the two fields may provide important inspirations. In the following two parts of this section, existing academic efforts in the two areas will be reviewed in detail.

3.1 Studies on Chinese to English Legal Translation

With the rapid economic development of China and the rapidly expanding exchanges between China and the rest of the world, there has been a phenomenal growth in academic studies on legal translation between Chinese and English, as well as in other related areas, such as the study of legal English for specific purposes.

The most prominent among the studies in this category so far is *New Approach to Legal Translation*, a seminal work by Šarčević that plays an instrumental role in spurring the current booming development of academic studies on legal translation in China (屈文生, 2009). In the book, the author Šarčević, professor of law from the Rijeka University of Croatia and one of the most prominent scholars in legal translation studies (屈文生, 2009), argued that legal translation, a once humble sub-area of translation study "snubbed for alleged inferiority" (Šarčević, 1997: 1) was actually playing a crucial role in today's world. She went on to enumerate the factors causing variations among corresponding legal terms of different jurisdictions, and put forward a number of methods for addressing such variations, including lexical expansion, descriptive paraphrases and definitions, as well as using neutral terms, borrowings, literal equivalents and coinages. What is especially noteworthy is the fact that she went beyond the translation of legal terminology in her studies: She suggested that legal translation should not be treated as merely trans-coding but a dual communicative process of legal transfer and language transfer (Šarčević, 1997: 147). Legal translation requires equivalence of language function as well as legal function. Although this book is based on the translation of legal documents among European Union countries and does not directly deal with the translating of Chinese legal texts, it has provided important inspiration to many Chinese researchers (杜金榜, 张福, 袁亮, 2004; 屈文生, 2008, 2009 and 2010), who in turn put forward a host of inspiring solutions to the translation of Chinese legal texts, including the famous three-fold principle by Du Jinbang (杜金榜), a prominent forensic language scholar of China, namely, "putting law before language; seeking common ground while reserving differences and using existing similar terms and expressions in the target language whenever possible".

Another inspiring monograph on legal translation is *Translating Law* by Deborah Cao (屈文生), in which Cao reviewed the characteristics of the legal language (normative, performative, technical and indeterminative), the qualifications of a competent legal translator (translational language competence, translational knowledge competence and translational strategic competence), and the translating of different types of legal texts. The author quotes freely examples from bilingual or even multilingual jurisdictions, e. g. , Hong Kong, Canada and Switzerland. The discussion of the legal translation in Hong Kong, where both English and Chinese are adopted as working languages in legal affairs, is especially relevant to China.

Besides publications by overseas scholars on legal translation in general, in the first category are also a host of works by China-based scholars. Among them, Chen Zhongcheng, a long-time researcher and practitioner of legal translation across English, Japanese, Russian and Chinese, is among the earliest scholars in China to pay serious attention to the study of legal translation after the legal system of China was rehabilitated in the late 1970s. In his delightful work, *Window on Legal Translation* (《法窗译话》)(陈忠诚, 1992), a collection of witty essays on legal translation between Chinese and English, he compared and contrasted many English legal terms with their Chinese counterparts, and put forward many translation tactics that are highly useful to frontline translators.

Following the example of this learned preacher and practitioner of legal translation, many other Chinese scholars are turning their attention to legal translation, which reflects the phenomenal expansion in the exchanges between China and the rest of the world. As a result, many insightful works emerged, dealing with specific aspects of Chinese to English legal translation, such as the translation of the titles of certain Chinese laws and regulations (顾维忱, 张军英, 2007; 辛谷, 2003), the translation of specific legal terms or usages, for example, the translation of deictic words (李楠, 2005), the translation of specific legal terms like "出让" (张武保, 2000), the translation of specific legislative texts, including the Constitution of the People's Republic of China, the Contract Law of the People's Republic of China, economic and trade laws, etc. (范晶波, 2010; 刘法公, 2001; 杜金榜, 张福, 袁亮, 2004).

Some other Chinese scholars, on the basis of such studies of micro aspects of legal translation, approached legal translation as a whole. The most noteworthy among them are Teng Chao and Kong Feiyan. In their book published in

2008, *English-Chinese Legal Translation: Theory and Practice* (滕超, 孔飞燕), the two authors not only discussed the features of legal language, but also elaborated on both the macro translation strategies (the different types of legal texts and the purposes of their translation) and the micro translation tactics (translation of legal terms and punctuation marks). What is particularly noteworthy is that this book adopted the German functionalist approach, especially the Skopos Theory, which has attracted the attention of both practitioners and theorists of translation for the purpose of international communication.

Another book that deals with the Chinese to English translation in an all-round way is *Legal Texts and Leal Translation*, the brainchild of Li Kexing and Zhang Xinhong, who put forward the principles, strategies and tactics of translation as well as a host of highly practical legal text models and translation models. A third book in this respect is Sun Wanbiao's *A Course in the Translation of Legal Documents* (孙万彪, 2004). This book is based on the evolution of a virtual company, including its initiation, incorporation, management, insolvency and bankruptcy as well as virtual litigation and other legal proceedings related to the company, and therefore is highly relevant to the study of translation of legal documents in connection with the business community.

Furthermore, as part of their publications, some Chinese scholars have made insightful studies on the Chinese to English translation of some types of legal documents. For example, Jia Wenbo included "the translation of official documents on business and trade" as a separate chapter of his book, *On Applied Translation: A Functionalist Approach* (贾文波, 2004), and elaborated on the feasibility of applying the German functionalism in the theory and practice of applied translation, legal translation included.

However, as far as the data collected by the author in this book are concerned, the existing academic studies on Chinese to English translation of legal documents are primarily focused on the traditional hard legal texts, and to be more specific, major laws, such as the Constitution, Civil Law, Criminal Law, Company Law, etc., as well as contracts, court documents, etc., but seldom involved in any discussion of the vast amount of documents known as administrative regulations, government circulars, judicial interpretations. Such legal documents, though usually not on a par with constitution and major laws in terms of priority or applicability, are legislations in their own right, and make up for the majority of legal documents (for example, while between 1976 and 1998, the National People's Congress of China adopted more than 337 laws, local People's congresses and governments issued as many as 6,000 administrative regulations). It is then unfair that so little attention is paid to the translation thereof.

In addition, all existing studies in this field are either focused on the translation of Chinese "hard legal texts", as is defined in Section 1.2 of the present book, i.e., legislations, legal instruments such as contracts and agreements and academic publications on law, or focused on the English to Chinese translation of foreign hard legal texts into Chinese, especially those in the west world. The legal texts studied in such academic undertakings are primarily for the benefit of an elite section of the society, namely, the legal professionals, scholars and business people engaged in the international trade. Important as they are in the Chinese legal system, hard legal texts are unfortunately beyond the reach of many Chinese citizens with the necessary training, and it is reasonable to assume that the translations of such hard legal texts would also pose daunting challenges to the typical targeted English reader, who may be "safely assumed to know little about China... and is a high school diploma holder" ["设想读者对中国一无所知，绝对没有错……（读者）具有高中毕业文化水平……"]（黎信，2009: 22), given the highly technical and complex nature of such legal texts and their translations. On the other hand, translation of soft legal texts, such as law-themed media reports and literary works, which are more reader-friendly, has been unfortunately given the cold shoulder in academic studies, although it may play a more effective role in providing the vast majority of the intended readers with information on China's legal system.

3.2 Studies on Translation for International Communication

Another field closely related to the present research is the study on the translation for international communication, as is defined in Section 1.2 of the book. As a matter of fact and as its name suggests, the theme of the present book,

Chinese to English translation of soft legal texts in the context of international communication of China's legal system, is actually a branch of the study on translation for international communication, which itself is an emerging field of study in China in the era of rejuvenation of China and globalization. Although according to the data available, there is yet to be any academic study on the Chinese to English translation of soft legal texts in the context of international communication of China's legal system, some of the findings of the existing studies on translation for China's international communication may provide important inspirations for the present research and form part of its ground work.

3. 2. 1 An Overview of Studies on Translation for the International Communication of China

Compared with traditional fields in translation study, such as study on the translation of literary works, or even that on the science and technology translation, the study of translation for international communication is a relative newcomer. For example, a search in the online catalogue system of China National Library (the third largest library in the world① with a collection of over 29 million volumes and 7. 45 million entries in its electronic catalogue by the end of the year 2010②) with the word "translation" as the key word turns up as many as 6,288 results, of which 2,636 are monographs on translation and 2,866 are graduation books on translation by candidates for master's and doctor's degrees, while a similar search with the words "translation for international communication" as keywords retrieved a pitiable 36 results, of which only one is monograph and the majority of the rest are books and thesis.

Searches with Chinese words closely associated with translation for international communication fared equally bad: for example, a search with the words "international communication" turned up 137 results, most of which are collec-

① *National library, world's 3rd largest*, retrieved from www. china. org. cn/china/national/2008 - 09/10/content_16423963_2. htm.

② Data retrieved from the official website of China National Library at www. nlc. gov. cn/dsb_footer/gygt/ghgy/.

tions of essays and memoirs of veteran translators and journalists and graduation theses and books in recent years, another search taking "journalistic translation (新闻翻译)" fared slightly better, getting 92 results, 65 of which are graduation theses and books and 14 monographs. In comparison, the humble science and technology translation is dealt with by 169 different academic undertakings, of which 128 are monographs. Perhaps more meaningful is the fact that the first ever Chinese academic attempt at the theme "translation for international communication" appeared as late as in the year 1999; in contrast, the first such attempt on the study on science and technology translation appeared in 1973.

Judging by the above figures, it can be said that serious academic interest in translation for international communication is a new albeit important phenomenon. The study of translation for international communication in China is still in its infancy: It still lacks a well-developed framework, with even the English translation of its very name, "外宣翻译", still open to debate. Most of the existing studies are still essentially written reflections of translation practitioners and remain to be crystallized into theoretical findings. The variety of media and languages studies is still rather limited, most of them tending to focus on the micro level, i. e., the translation of certain types of texts, specific texts or even words, many of the existing studies are not based on proper methodology (仇贤根, 2010: 33).

3.2.2 Existing Publications on Translation for International Communication: Importance, Inspirations and Insights

In general, existing publications on translation (especially Chinese to English) for international communication purposes may be divided into two categories according to whether they are reflections, memoirs or sum-ups of experienced journalists, translators and administrators involved in China's international communication efforts or the results of formal academic efforts of scholars engaged in studies on China's efforts to introduce itself to the rest of the world. In the following parts of this section, the leading publications of the two categories will be reviewed respectively.

The most prominent publication in the first category is probably the 2009

Chinese monograph *Theory for International Communication—A Collection of Works on Translation Research* (《对外传播翻译研究论文集》) of the late Mr. Shen Suru (沈苏儒, 1919—2009), a veteran journalist, translator, editor and administrator engaged in China's international communication undertaking. This book, which was jointly collected and compiled by the Center for International Communication Studies of the China International Publishing Group (one of the most important and by far the most time-honored specialized international communication agencies of the People's Republic of China, where Mr. Shen worked as "a senior language expert"①) and the multilingual magazine *China Today*, where Mr. Shen served as Deputy Editor-in-chief for many years, is a collection of Mr. Shen's "published essays on international communication theories and on translation from 1984 to 2009"②, and is viewed by his former colleagues as the "crystallization of many years of hard work" of Mr. Shen. As its title suggests, essays in this book fall into two categories, namely, those on international communication and those on translation. However, the distinction between the two types of essays is not absolute, because for Mr. Shen, international communication and translation (in the case of Mr. Shen, Chinese to English translation) are deeply entwined—the quality of translation directly decides the success or failure of international communication (沈苏儒, 2009: 354). On the other hand, translation for international communication must serve its intended purposes, i.e., to facilitate such communication. Therefore, translation for international communication is different from translation in the traditional sense in that it enjoys greater "flexibility" so that the translated texts will be readily acceptable by the intended readers and thereby achieve their intended purpose. In so doing, the long-held doctrine of "literal faithfulness (to the orig-

---

① China International Publishing Group (CIPG), whose motto is "we present China to the world", "was founded in 1949 with a mission to introduce China to foreign countries through books, magazines and websites. CIPG has over 20 subsidiaries as well as 12 overseas branches located in the United States, Britain, Germany, Belgium, Russia, Egypt, Mexico, Japan and Hong Kong, constituting a conglomerate of foreign language publishing and marketing". Information here is retrieved from the official website of the China International Publishing Group at www.cipg.org.cn/jjgl/.

② *Forever Cherish the Memory of Mr. Shen Suru, Honorary Council Member of Our Foundation*, eulogy released by the China Soong Ching Ling Foundation on July 13, 2009 for the passing away of Mr. Shen, retrieved from the official website of the Foundation at http://sclf.cri.cn/1/2009/07/13/2s1189.htm.

inal texts)" should be done away with (沈苏儒, 2009: 30). Topics of the essays in this collection range from strategies in international communication of China and translation for such international communication, such as ways to improve the overall quality of news reports targeting foreign audiences (沈苏儒, 2009: 128 – 135), specific tactics in international communication, such as the proper use of facts (沈苏儒, 2009: 38 – 43) and figures (沈苏儒, 2009: 44 – 48), the importance of providing background information to the recipients (沈苏儒, 2009: 31 – 37), comments on the merits of specific publications (沈苏儒, 2009: 82 – 86, 沈苏儒, 2009: 142 – 144). These insightful articles, which are based on years' experiences of Mr. Shen and his colleagues, provide important inspirations to today's international communication practitioners of China (translators included, of course). In particular, the following five principles put forward by Mr. Shen (沈苏儒, 2009: 129 – 131) on improving "overseas reporting" of China are still highly relevant today:

(1) Be aware of the differences between the domestic communication and international communication and keep away from the principles and practices that apply to domestic communication only. In so doing, the international communication practitioners should: ①adopt the perspective of the average recipients instead of that of the government leaders and officials; ②view news reporting to overseas audiences as a truthful description of life (in a broader sense) instead of government work summaries, plans or reports; ③NOT adopt the lofty attitude that their role is to lecture their audience; instead, they should view themselves as service providers; ④give priority to the human factor in their reporting and give their work a human face. [摆脱对内宣传的模式和影响，方法包括：①从官方的、领导的角度转变为普通人、老百姓的角度。②从工作总结、工作计划、工作报告转变为生活的描述（这里说的生活是广义的）。③从教育者转变为传播者、服务者。④从见物不见人转变为人是第一位的，物从属于人。(沈苏儒, 2009: 129)]

(2) Do not force your opinions on the readers. Let the facts speak for themselves and let the readers draw their own conclusions on the basis of facts. Refrain from any exaggeration or falsification, because they are repulsive to the readers. [让事实说话，让读者自己下结论。越是说得天花乱坠，越容易产生负面效应。(沈苏儒, 2009: 129, 130)]

(3) Make sure that your reporting is readily comprehensible by the intend-

ed audience. Keep in mind of the warning of the British journalist Felix Greene to Chinese international communication practitioners that "foreigners are not Chinese", i. e. , the vast cultural differences between China and the target countries must be taken into account in China's efforts to present itself to the world, and necessary modification must be done to the original texts in the translation process, including adding necessary interpretations for culture-loaded matters and leaving out information that is not relevant to the theme of the reporting. [必须使国外受众能够理解。不可忘记"外国人不是中国人";"写对外报道,要随时想一想外国人懂不懂"……"一些有关中国特殊国情的问题……必须解释清楚","对于外国人难懂而又与主题无关的内容,不妨略去"。(沈苏儒, 2009: 130)]

(4) Highlighting the key points and unique features of what is reported and avoid blindly following stereotypes. [突出重点,抓住特色,避免一般化。(沈苏儒, 2009: 131)]

(5) Be concise, direct and plain in style and avoid loading your writing with florid and fancy but empty phrases. [做到"短平快"。文章一定要短,文字力求简明,主题明确;文字平实,不要堆砌辞藻;快速进入正题。(沈苏儒, 2009: 131)]

Another prominent work in the first category of publications on the international communication of China is the 2009 monograph *A Practical Guide for International News Reporting in English* (《英语对外新闻报道指南》) by Li Xin, pen name of Li Zhurun, a senior journalist with Xinhua News Agency, China's state news agency, and Guest Professor of the Department of Journalism under the School of English and International Studies of the Beijing Foreign Studies University, one of the most prestigious higher education institutions of foreign languages and international studies in China. This book, like that by Mr. Shen, is based on the author's rich experiences as an on-the-field translator-journalist. However, if the book of Mr. Shen is a collection of essays, book reviews and prefaces written by a veteran Chinese practitioner of international communication over a period of 25 years that primarily intends to provide insight and inspiration on the strategic level, this book by Mr. Li is "an ideal textbook for aspirant international journalists of China (一部对外新闻报道的最佳实用教材)" (黎

信，2009：Ⅱ) that is highly informative, practical, inspiring and timely (黎信，2009：Ⅱ－Ⅲ).

Starting with a brief description of modern journalistic English texts, their difference between Chinese texts of the same category, and the special warning to aspirant international journalists to presume that their target readers know little, if not nothing about China, this book goes on to discuss the writing of various types of journalistic texts in English, including hard news, feature reports and opinion articles and provide many practical tips along the way. The suggestions put forward by this book, echo the five principles proposed in Mr. Shen's book, and goes further by providing specific tactics in such aspects as how to inspire the reader's interests, how to tailor journalistic texts by Chinese authors who are not native users of the English language to the needs of their intended readers, so that will become more readily acceptable and comprehensible. In general, like Mr. Shen's book, this monograph also stresses the necessity of conforming to the journalistic and linguistic norms in the culture of the intended readers.

Aside from monographs, a number of articles published in academic journals and magazines by journalists, translators, editors and administrators engaged in China's international communication efforts also provide this book with valuable inspirations. One of the most widely cited article of this kind is the 2004 article *Addressing Difficult Translation Issues in China's International Communication According to "Three In-line-with Principles* (English translation by the author of the book from Chinese original:《坚持“外宣三贴近”原则，处理好外宣翻译中的难点问题》) by Huang Youyi, another veteran in the field of China's international communication who holds the office of Vice President of the International Federation of Translators①, vice president of China International

① The International Federation of Translators "is an international federation of translators' associations which are located in nearly 50 countries throughout the world. Through its member associations, FIT represents the moral and material interests of over 60,000 translators on all five continents. FIT is a strictly non-political organization of professional translators. As a non-governmental federation, FIT enjoys Category A status with UNESCO and maintains close contacts with many other international organizations", in accordance with the report titled *Huang Youyi reelected FIT Vice President* (http://www.china.org.cn/2008－08/03/content_16124415.htm) retrieved from the website of the China Internet Information Center, which is an authorized government portal site to China, and is published under the auspices of the State Council Information Office and the China International Publishing Group (CIPG) in Beijing.

Publishing Group, president of the China Internet Information Center and vice chairman and secretary-general of the Translators Association of China. This article argues that aside from the principles applicable to translation in general, translation for international communication, as a branch of translation, must also abide another three principles that specifically governs this field, namely, translation for international communication must be in line with the actual state of China's development, in line with the intended recipients' need for information on China and in line with the thinking patterns of such recipients [除去所有翻译工作都需要遵循的“信、达、雅”标准之外，外宣翻译……更需要运用“外宣翻译三贴近”（贴近中国发展的实际，贴近国外受众对中国信息的需求，贴近国外受众的思维习惯）]. The author went on to caution translators against mechanical and rigid word-for-word and sentence-for-sentence literal translation in international communication and suggested that proper "modifications" be made to the original Chinese texts, including deletion, insertion of necessary background information, in light of the thinking patterns of the intended target recipients of such translations. These principles, proposed in this article, collectively referred to as the three in-line-with principles, which echo with the above two monographs and are widely quoted by many scholars and translation practitioners, having been widely accepted as established guidelines for translation for China's international communication.

Other senior translators, journalists and editors have also published articles and essays dealing with translation for China's international communication, whose topic range from translation as a whole, to the translation of certain types of texts, even specific words and expressions. For example, Yan Wei (闫威), senior journalist in *Beijing Review*, China's leading multilingual news weekly, pointed out that translation for international communication is not translation in the traditional sense, instead, it is a combination of edition and translation. The translation must, in light of the three in-line-with principles, process the original texts on both the micro and macro levels by making bold deletions and enhancements in the translation process, so that the target language text will achieve equivalence in effect with the source language text (闫威, 2011). In another article published in 2010, Ms. Jia Yuling (贾毓玲), senior translator with the Central Compilation and Translation Bureau, whose international communication arm specializes in translating important works and documents of the central authorities of China[①], shared with the readers her experiences in translating documents of the Central authorities of China. Ms. Jia emphasized the importance of thorough understanding of the Chinese originals of the documents to be translated and extra-language factors, such as sufficient background information concerning the documents under translation, and warned the translator against mechanically transferring the structure of the source language text into the target language text.

Furthermore, some articles in this category put the translation for international communication under a microscope, so to speak, dealing exclusively with the translation of certain words. In an article published on the basis of many concrete examples, Mr. Wang Pingxing (王平兴), senior journalist and language expert with the international department of the Xinhua News Agency, discussed the translation of a number of important words in Chinese politics and argued that for the translated versions of the words to be readily understandable and acceptable by the intended recipients, they must conform with the language norms of the countries or regions where such recipients are from. Notably, the author emphasized the role of parallel texts (see section 1. 2. 6 of the present book) in improving the quality and reader acceptability of translation (王平兴, 2010). Another article by Xie Qiao, senior translator and deputy editor-in-chief with the board of English service of China Radio International, the national external broadcasting station of China, specifically discussed the translation of the Chinese word "劳动 (literally, work or labor)" in China's international communication, and elaborated on how mistranslation of this seemingly simple word may cause confusion or misunderstanding, if the economic, cultural, ideological and religious differences between China and the countries or regions that the intended recipients of the translation fail to be given due consideration.

To sum up, the first category of publications on translation for international

---

① In accordance with a profile of the Bureau on the website of the China Internet Information Center, *The work of the Central Compilation and Translation Bureau* released on December 9, 2010 at www. china. org. cn/china/2010 - 12/09/content_21509523. htm.

communication is the crystallization of the experiences and expertise of veteran translators, journalists, editors and administrators involved in China's efforts to present itself to the world, and the suggestions, advice, warnings and cautions that they put forward are of important value to the present research.

With the rapid development of China and the ongoing globalization process that brings the world smaller than ever, China has become keenly aware of the need to present itself to the rest of the world in a balanced and fair way, so as to dispel the misperception of China and create a favorable environment for its development and closer integration into the international communication. Hence, recent decades have witnessed the remarkable intensification of China's international efforts, which, in turn, have greatly spurred academic interest in this emerging branch of translation studies. The resulting publications fall into the second category, i. e., those formal academic publications backed up by certain theories.

Like those in the first category, publications in the second category may also be divided into those dealing with translation for international communication on a macro level, i. e., its overall features and feasible strategies, and those on a micro level, i. e., specific translation tactics, the translation of specific texts, phrases or words. However, publications in this category will be primarily reviewed according to their theoretical basis and findings.

First, some publications deal with translation for international communication within the framework of certain translation theories. For example, in their 2007 article published in *Shanghai Journal of Translators*, Jia Hui (贾卉) and Huang Hui (黄慧) elaborated on the application of constructivist translatology in what they called "external publicity translation" (which is synonymous with translation for international communication as defined in the book), and argued that translators should have a thorough analysis of the source language text before they set out to translate it, that interpretive tactics should be adopted for culturally-loaded words and expressions and translators must see to that the end products of their efforts must conform to the norms of the target language in terms of style and meaning (黄慧, 贾卉, 2007). Another example in point is the 2005 article of Yuan Xiaoning (袁晓宁). This article, based on the theory of the British translation theorist Peter Newmark, proposed that a communicative translation approach should be adopted and that the target language text, especially its effectiveness and acceptability in the target language culture must be given top priority (袁晓宁, 2005). A third article (胡芳毅, 贾文波, 2010) explored the political and ideological aspects of translation for China's international communication according to the arguments put forward by André Lefevere (1992) and defined China's translation for international communication is in essence rewriting according to ideological difference between China and the countries and regions where the intended recipients are from so that the translations will be acceptable to such recipients.

Notably, the German functionalist approach to translation, especially the Skopos Theory, is receiving increasing attention in academic studies on translation for international communication, partially because this approach is highly compatible with the accumulated experiences and expertise of practitioners of China's international communication, such as the three in-line-with principles. For example, on the basis of his experience of translating the Chinese TV newsreels sent to the Cable News Network (CNN) by a local television station in China, Wu Zixuan (吴自选) discussed the applicability of the functionalist approach to translation, especially the Skopos Theory to China's international communication, and argued that this approach provides strong theoretical support for such translation tactics as deletion, rewriting and interpretive translation employed in China's international communication (吴自选, 2005). Another example in case is the 2010 book of Xiao Qun (肖群), *A Study of Revolution-Enrichment Tourist Publicity C-E Translation: Problems and Strategies—From the Perspective of Functionalism*, in which "adequacy", the standard for translation quality evaluation in the functionalist approach is adopted to analyze the existing errors in the translation of tourism promotion materials for regions associated with China's revolutions between 1920s and 1940s. The book concludes that the functionalist approach allows more flexibility in translation tactics and even "deviation" from the long-held fidelity principle, as long as the intended translation purpose is fulfilled, and "translation brief" [a term under the functionalist approach referring to the "definition of the communicative purpose for which the translation is needed. The ideal brief provides explicit or implicit information about the intended text function(s), the target-text addressee(s), the medium over which it will be transmitted, the prospective place and time and, if necessary, motive of production or reception of the text" (Nord, 2001a: 137)] plays a crucial role in translation, and that translation errors in the translation of this specific range of texts may be divided into those on the pragmatic, cultural and linguistic levels.

A number of other publications tackled the translation for international communication of China from the perspective of communication theories, the most in-depth and comprehensive of which is the book *C-E Translation for Global Communication: From a Perspective of Communication Studies with a Case Study on China Today* by Yang Xuelian (杨雪莲, 2010). As its name suggests, this book approaches the translation for international communication of China from the perspective of communication studies, proceeding from the argument that "communication and translation share the nature of dissemination and exchanging of information" (2010: Ⅻ), and "translation is a purposeful communication that overcomes the interruption of noise and thus achieves the expected communication effect among the receivers" (2010: XⅢ). Within this framework, the book reviewed the translation practice of the English edition of the monthly magazine *China Today*, "a pioneering model of English periodicals in China's international communication" (杨雪莲, 2010: XIX) at both the lexical and the discourse level, and found that on the former level foreignization is the prevailing approach so as to preserve the flavor of the original as much as possible while on the latter level domestication is often adopted so as to make the translation more readable and acceptable to the readers (杨雪莲, 2010), and pointed out that this proper combination of foreignization and domestication is an important factor behind the success of the magazine (杨雪莲, 2010). In particular, this book advocates the "foreignization" approach on the cultural level as a way to promote "intercultural communication" (杨雪莲, 2010: 7) and cautions against the tendency to overuse the domestication approach in a bid to accommodate to the perceived needs of the target readers, arguing that the two approaches must be properly combined and foreignization should be adopted whenever and wherever it does not affect the readability and acceptability of the translation (杨雪莲, 2010: 36).

All in all, works on translation for China's international communication are increasing in number and becoming more systematic in theoretical framework. However, in the context of the book, they are either all-inclusive, i. e. , discussing the Chinese to English translation in China's global communication in general, or are specifically-targeted, discussing the translation of certain types of documents, specific texts or even terms and expressions. No existing study has ever approached the translation of legal texts from the perspective of international communication.

3.3 Summary of This Chapter

In the previous two sections in this chapter, both the practice and theoretical studies related to the Chinese to English translation of soft legal texts in the context of international communication of China's legal system are reviewed. According to the data collected by the author of the present book after extensive research, there is yet to be an academic effort at the Chinese to English translation for the purpose of the international communication of China's legal system that targets both the elite community of legal professionals as well as the vast majority of potential audiences of China's international communication, who in many cases are not familiar with the legal systems of their own countries or jurisdictions, let alone the legal system of China, which still remains little-known and much-misunderstood emerging power. In view of this, the present research attempts to fill this void and explore the problems with such translation within a systematic theoretical framework and propose solutions, if somewhat tentative ones, to such translations problems.

Also, many important inspirations have been drawn from the systematic review of both the practice and theory of translation for China's international communication. It is particularly noteworthy that there seem to be remarkable similarities or even correspondence between the principles and rules summarized by seasoned external publicity practitioners of China and arguments of scholars of the German functionalist school, such as the principle of receiver-centeredness and the necessity of providing necessary background information. In the following chapter, the German functionalist approach will be discussed in detail and compared with the rules and principles drawn up veteran Chinese journalists and translators, in the hope of finding the relations between the two and possibly providing a systematic theoretical guideline for the international publicity-related translation of China.

Chapter Four Theoretical Framework of the Present Research

In the present book, German functionalism is adopted as the foundation of its theoretical framework, which will be demonstrated and proved in the present chapter, German functionalism is in perfect agreement with the rules and principles drawn up by generations of translators, editors, journalists and administrators engaged in the "international communication of China" (which is the background theme of the book) on the basis of their many years' experience and practice, and therefore, it can be said that the relevance and applicability of the German functional approach to translation in the international communication of China has been confirmed. In turn, as a well-developed and tested school of translation studies, the German functionalism can provide systematic theoretical guidance to both practitioners and researcher of Chinese to English legal text translation in the context of the international communication of China.

4.1 The German Functionalist Approach to Translation Studies: A Profile

In the context of the book, the German functionalism in translation studies refers to the school of translation theory first proposed and formed by a number of German translation scholars, the most prominent among whom are Katharina Reiss, Hans Vermeer and Christiane Nord. The 30-odd years since its birth in the 1970s have witnessed phenomenal development of the school of translation studies. However, since most of the publications of the leading figures of this school of translation study are in German, the influence of German functionalism remained rather limited. In view of this, Christiane Nord, the leading figure of German functionalism today after the retirement of its pioneers like Katharina Reiss, translated her 1988 work *Text Analysis in Translation: Theory, Methodology and Didactic Application of a Model for Translation-Oriented Text Analysis* into English in 1991 (the second edition of this translation was published by the Foreign Language Teaching and Research Press in China in 2006) and later wrote another book *Translation as a Purposeful Activity*: *Functional Approach Explained* directly in English in 1997 (which was published by the Shanghai Foreign Language Education Press in China in 2001) to introduce functionalism to a wider readership. On the basis of the two publications as well as some other articles and books, the main view points of German functionalism will be introduced, including the translational action, the Skopos theory, translation brief, adequacy as the standard for translation quality assessment, the selection of translation strategy and translation problem solutions, and the role of auxiliary texts in helping translators achieve translation adequacy.

4.1.1 Translational Action and Translation

Based on the action theory, German functionalists proposed the theory of translational action. In German functionalism, "translational action" is a generic term that is "designed to cover all forms of intercultural transfer, including those which do not involve any source or target texts", while translation is defined as "in the wider sense, any translational action where a source text is transferred into a target culture and language" (Nord, 2001a: 141). In this sense, translation can be viewed as a form of translational action based on a source text that may consist of verbal and/or non-verbal elements such as illustrations, plans, tables (Nord, 2001a: 11).

The relation between translational action and translation in the traditional sense may be summarized as follows:

First, translational action refers the range of things that translators actually do, while translation refers to what translators do when they are rendering texts.

Second, while translation always involves some kind of source text, translational action does not necessarily involve source text and may involve giving advice and perhaps even warning against communicating in the intended way (Nord, 2001a: 17).

The relations between action, interaction, translational action and translation may be shown in a more readily understandable manner by the figure below (Nord, 2001a: 18):

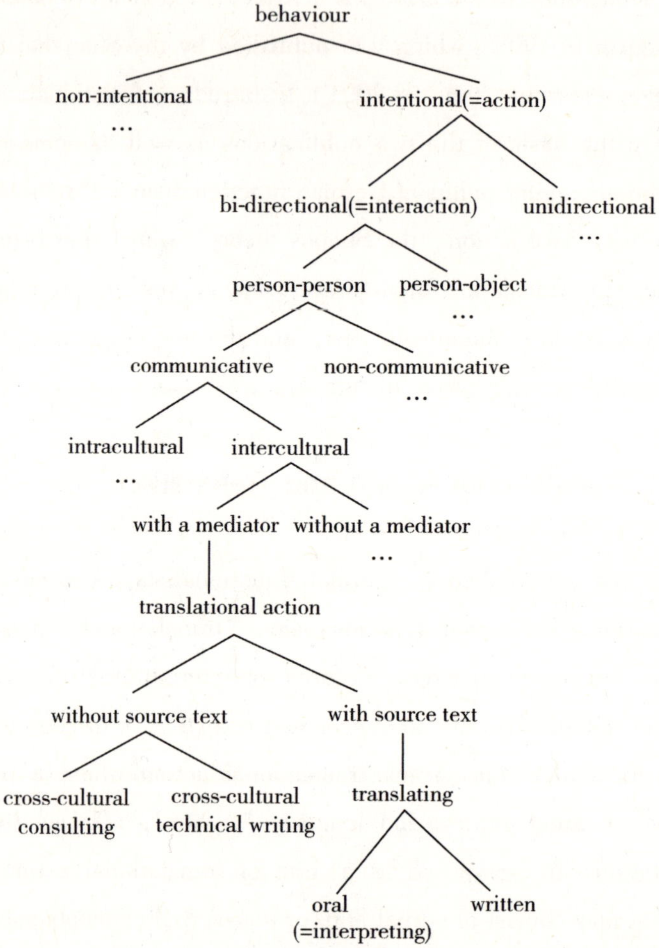

Figure 1 Translation as a Form of Mediated Intercultural Interaction

According to the translational action theory, translating, the action side of translation, is viewed as: ①a form of translational interaction; ②intentional action; ③interpersonal interaction; ④communicative action; ⑤intercultural action; and ⑥text-processing action. The six features attributed to translation by German functionalists will be discussed in the following parts of this section.

4.1.1.1 Translating as a Form of Translational Interaction

Translation is deemed as a form of translational interaction because through their translational actions, translators make it possible for members of different cultural communities to effectively interact with each other, who otherwise would be unable to communicate with each other because of a lack of common ground in terms of verbal and non-verbal behavior. In this sense, translators help to bridge the gap between the two sides of the communication, namely, the "sender" and "receiver" of communicative signs who belong to different cultures.

4.1.1.2 Translating as Intentional Interaction

German functionalist school of translation studies views translation as intentional interaction because translation is "*intended*① to change an existing state of affairs (minimally, the inability of certain people to communicate with each other). There may be further intentions of a more strictly communicative nature, such as to inform the target addressees about something the source-text sender has to say" (Nord, 2001a: 19).

It should be noted that the intentionality of translation is more often associated with the "initiator" of the translation process (the initiator is a new player introduced into the translation process by the German functionalist, who, together with other figures involved, will be explained in detail in the following section) than with the translator (Mord, 2001a: 19). This new role added to the translation process concerns the third feature of translating in German functionalism: translating as interpersonal interaction.

4.1.1.3 Translating as Interpersonal Interaction

The introduction of new agents into the translation process is one of the features that distinguish the German functionalist approach to translation studies from other translation studies approaches (仲伟合, 钟钰, 1999). Proceeding from the functionalist description of translation as an intercultural communication and a form of translational action, German functionalists identify a total of six roles involved in the translation process, namely: the initiator (the client), commissioner of translation, the translator, the source text producer, and the receiver/

① Italicized by the author of the book from which these remarks are quoted.

addressee of the target text, and the final user of the target text (Nord, 2001a: 20); in contrast, other approaches to translation studies only include the original text producer, the translator and receiver of target text as participants in the translation process (Nord, 2001a: 20). In the following part of this section, the six roles in the translation process will be introduced.

As has been mentioned in the part on translating as intentional interaction, the initiator is the person (or group or institution, as the case may be) that initiates the translation process and determines its course by defining the purpose for which the target text is needed. The initiator should be distinguished from the commissioner of translation. While the initiator is the party who needs the target text the commissioner is the party that commissions the translator to produce the target text for a particular purpose and addressee; in other words, the commissioner does not necessarily needs the target text, even though it may influence "the production of the target text, perhaps by demanding a particular text format or terminology" (Nord, 2001a: 20).

The translator is deemed by German functionalists as a crucial role in the translation process, because "the translator is ostensibly the expert in translational action and should be responsible both for carrying out the commissioned task and for ensuring the result of the translation process" (Nord, 2001a: 21). In the translation process, the translator first acts as a receiver of both the "translation brief" (essentially the translation commissioner's instructions; it is an important concept in the German functionalist approach to translation studies and will be discussed in detail in the following parts of this section) and the source text. After agreeing with the commissioner on the conditions involved, the translator produces a target text that he or she regards as functional, i. e., it meets the demands of the translation brief. The translator's tasks may be summed up as follows:

(1) Analyze the acceptability and viability of the translation brief in legal, economic or ideological terms.

(2) Check whether the translation is really needed.

(3) Specify the activities required for carrying out the brief.

(4) Perform a translational action, which may result in a target text, per-

haps a short summary of the source text or, in special cases, in advising the client not to have the source text translated because a translation would not serve the intended purpose (Nord, 2001a: 21).

It can be inferred from the above "job description" of a translator that in the functionalist approach, the translator is allowed greater flexibility in deciding which approach would work better in the given situation, or even whether the translation is actually viable or necessary. In this sense, German functionalism views translators as experts in intercultural communication and as responsible partners in communication events, not as secondary, mechanical scribes (Gentzler, 2001: 71), or a humble and poorly-paid "bilingual typist" (Morris, 1995: 238). The translator is empowered and elevated to equal status with authors, editors, and clients, and is entrusted to make appropriate, rational decisions that best realize the intended inter-cultural communication.

Source-text producer is "the person, group or institution that is responsible for the textual production of the source text" (Schjoldager, 2008: 161). However, it should be noted that the source text is not necessarily produced for the purpose of translation.

The next role in the translation process is the target-text receiver, who is the addressee of the translation. The specification of the target-text receiver is required as an indispensable part of the translation brief, because "information about the target-text addressee (such as his or her socio-cultural background, expectations, sensitivity or world knowledge) is of crucial importance for the translator, who should insist on receiving as many details as possible from the commissioner" (Nord, 2001a: 23).

As has been noted in previous parts of this book, the addressee must be distinguished from the receiver: While the former is the prospective receiver seen from the text producer's standpoint; the latter, the receiver, on the other hand, is the person, group or institution that actually reads or listens to the text after it has been produced (Nord, 2001a: 22).

The last of the six roles is the target-text user, who is the one who actually uses the target text.

So far, all the six roles in the translation process in the German functionalist approach to translation studies have been introduced. It is necessary to reiterate here that two or more of the six roles may be fulfilled by one and the same person. For example, a Chinese writer who entrusts a translator to render a Chinese novel that he writes into English is both the initiator and source-text producer in the translation process.

4.1.1.4 Translating as a Communicative Action

As has been pointed out in section 4. 1. 1. 1, translation is also a form of communication and is carried out by signs. The producer and the receiver of such signs must have some kind of agreement about the meaning of the signs used, so as to achieve the intended goal of translational communication (Nord, 2001a: 22-23). However, as signs are conventional and culture-specific (Nord, 2001a: 22), and the meaning associated with the signs are not necessarily the same for both the producer and the receiver. It is therefore advisable for the translator to exercise due caution when using signs that may be misinterpreted in the target language culture and derail such translational communication.

4.1.1.5 Translating as Intercultural Action

For German functionalists, translation takes place in concrete, definable situations that involve members of different cultures (Nord, 2001a: 24). In view of this, translating has to cross cultural boundaries and therefore is a cross-cultural action. Given the complexity of cultures and the vagueness between different cultural systems or sub-systems within cultures and the fact that culture boundary is marked by "rich points", which are "differences in behavior causing culture conflicts or communication breakdowns" (Nord, 2001a: 24-25), the translator would be well-advised and has to be aware of the rich points relevant to a particular translation task between different cultural groups or subgroups.

4.1.1.6 Translating as a Text-processing Action

German functionalists describe translation or translating as "a translational action based on some kind of text" (Nord, 2001a: 25). The term "some kind of text" in this definition indicates "a broad concept, combining verbal and non-verbal elements, situational clues and 'hidden' or presupposed information. The proportion of verbalized to non-verbalized text elements in a particular type of situation is culture-specific" (Nord, 2001a: 25).

In German functionalism, the role of the source text in translational action is radically different from earlier linguistic or equivalence-based translation theories. Source text is no longer considered as the first and foremost criterion for the translator's decisions, but just an offer of information. Any receiver (among them, the translator) chooses the items they regard as interesting, useful or adequate to the desired purposes. The chosen informational items are then transferred into the target culture in a way the translator believes appropriate for the given purpose. A translation is thus a new offer of information in the target culture about some information offered in the source culture and language (Nord, 2001a: 25 - 26).

It can be inferred from the above description of translation according to the German functionalist approach that achieving the intended or required purpose seems to be of the paramount importance in the translational action: It is both the starting point and ultimate goal. This purpose-orientated approach is known as the Skopos theory, which is arguably the most widely quoted view of the German functionalist school of translation study and will be discussed in detail in the following section.

4.1.2 The Skopos Theory

The Skopos Theory (German: Skopos Theorie) is a translation theory that is based on the translational action theory and "applies the notion of *Skopos* to translation" (Nord, 2001a: 27). According to this theory, the prime principle determining any translation process is the purpose (Skopos) of the overall translational action; in other words, the end justifies the means.

What, then, decides the translation Skopos? According to German functionalism, the Skopos of a translational action is decided by the translation client, i.e., the initiator of the translation process. Ideally, the initiator will provide the translator with as much information as possible on the target language text, including the function(s), addressees, time, place, occasion and medium of the intended communication. Such information constitutes a "translation brief", which is another important concept in German functionalism and in essence a detailed breakdown of the translation Skopos. In the following section, this concept will be discussed in detail.

4.1.2.1 Translation Brief

German functionalists define a translation brief (sometimes cited directly as "brief" for short) as the "definition of the communicative purpose for which the translation is needed. The ideal brief provides explicit or implicit information about the intended text function(s), the target-text addressee(s), the medium over which it will be transmitted, the prospective place and time and, if necessary, motive of production or reception of the text" (Nord, 2001a: 137).

In an ideal situation, the translation client is supposed to provide the translator with a clear translation brief. In actual translation practice, the client, not being an expert in intercultural communication and hence not aware of the importance of the translation brief, does not always provide the translator with a translation brief. Even if the client does, the translation brief may be too vague to be workable or even contain incorrect ideas. In both cases, the translator, as an expert on intercultural communication, should negotiate with the client on the translation Skopos and the translation brief. In addition, as has been pointed out in 4.1.1.3, the translator should also analyze the acceptability and viability of the translation brief from the perspective of legal, economic or ideological terms and even check whether the translation is really needed. All these responsibilities testify to the elevated status of the translator in the German functional approach to translation (Nord, 2001a: 30).

Crucial as it is, the translation brief itself does not directly tell the translator how to translate, such as what translation strategy to use or what translation type to choose. These decisions depend entirely on the translator's responsibility and competence (Nord, 2001a: 30), which will be discussed in subsequent parts of this chapter.

4.1.2.2 Three Translation Rules Under the Skopos Theory

According to the Skopos Theory, all translations should follow three rules, namely, the Skopos Rule, the Coherence Rule and the Fidelity Rule (仲伟合, 钟钰, 1999).

4.1.2.2.1 The Skopos Rule

The Skopos Rule is the top ranking rule for any translation: Translational action is determined by its Skopos, in other words, "the end justifies the means".

The Skopos rule provides a viable solution to a number of seemingly eternal dilemmas in translation studies, such as those of free translation vs. faithful translation, dynamic equivalence vs. formal equivalence, good interpreters vs. slavish translators, among others. According to the Skopos rule, whether a particular translation tasks requires free translation, faithful translation or something between the two extremes, actually depends "on the purpose for which the translation is needed" (Nord, 2001a: 29).

4.1.2.2.2 The Intra-textual Coherence Rule

According to the coherence rule, the target text produced through the translation process must be understandable to the receiver and that it should make sense in the communicative situation and culture in which it is received. The success or failure of a communicative interaction depends on whether "the receivers interpret it as being sufficiently coherent with their situation" (Nord, 2001a: 32).

4.1.2.2.3 The Inter-textual Coherence or Fidelity Rule

In German functionalism, the target text is viewed as "an offer of information formulated by a translator in a target culture and language about an offer of information formulated by someone else in the source culture and language" (Nord, 2001a: 32). It can be assumed that the target language text and source language text (two offers of information) should bear some kind of relationship. This relationship is termed as "inter-textual coherence" or "fidelity", and sometimes referred to as the "fidelity rule". The degree of "fidelity" may vary according to the translator's interpretation of the source text and on the translation Skopos (Nord, 2001a: 32).

The three rules are not equal in terms of priority. The intra-textual coherence rule and inter-textual rule are subject to the Skopos rule, and between themselves, the intra-textual rule takes precedence over the inter-textual coherence rule. For example, if the Skopos demands intratextual incoherence (as in the theatre of the absurd), the standard of intratextual coherence will not apply. If the Skopos requires a change of function, the inter-textual coherence will not apply; what will apply instead is the rule of "adequacy" (Nord, 2001a: 33), yet another important feature of German functionalism, which will be discussed in detail in the following section.

4.1.3 Adequacy and Equivalence

As has been noted in Section 4.1.1, an important feature of German functionalism is that it replaces the traditional concept of translation "equivalence" with a new concept, "adequacy", as the standard for assessing the quality of translation. Adequacy refers to the qualities of a target text with regard to the translation brief: The translation is deemed as adequate as long as it fulfills the requirements of the translation brief. However, the German functionalists do not discredit the notion "equivalence". Instead, German functionalists view "adequacy" as a superordinate concept of "equivalence". That is to say, equivalence is one form of "adequacy": "Equivalence means adequacy to a Skopos that requires that the target text serve the same communicative function or functions as the source text, thus preserving invariance of function between source and target text" (Nord, 2001a: 36). Therefore, it can be said that adequacy is a dynamic concept related to the process of translational action while equivalence is a static and result-oriented concept.

4.1.4 Achieving Translation Adequacy

So far in this introduction of German functionalism as the theoretical foundation of the book, the functionalist definition of translation, the translation roadmap—translation brief, and the translation quality assessment standard have been introduced. However, an important link in the translation process remains missing, namely, the identification of the translation strategy by which the translator achieves translation adequacy. As has been pointed out in the section on translation brief, in spite of its significance, the translation brief does not tell the translator the most appropriate translation strategy, the translator, for his part, must select the translation strategy through his responsibilities and competence. This question of how to translate is exactly what this section set out to solve.

4.1.4.1 Typology of Textual Functions

According to Nord, the most appropriate translation strategy for a specific translational action is determined by the intended function of the target language text (2001a: 39) and a comparison of the source language text and target language text according to the parameters listed in the translation brief, namely, the intended text function(s), the addressee(s), the (prospective) time and place of text reception, the medium over which the text will be transmitted, and the motive for the production or reception of the text (2001a: 62 - 63). In this process, the correct identification of the function(s) of the source and texts plays a crucial role.

Nord has proposed a "translation-oriented model of text functions", which consists of four basic functions—the referential function, the expressive function, the appellative function and the phatic function. The four functions may also be broken down into a number of sub-functions according to the way they are represented in texts and they concern specific translation problems (Nord, 2001a: 40).

The referential function involves (objective) reference to the objects and phenomena of the world. It may be analyzed according to the nature of the object or referent concerned. Main sub-functions under this function include informative, metalinguistic, metatextual, directive, didactic, etc (Nord, 2009).

The expressive function involves the expression of the sender's (subjective) attitudes or feelings towards the things and phenomena of the world. According to what is actually expressed, this function may be divided into sub-functions, chief among which are evaluative, emotive, ironical etc (Nord, 2001a: 41). According to Nord, this function is sender-oriented, i. e., the opinions expressed with regard to the referents are based on the value system of the sender, which may be different from that of the receiver, since such value systems are conditioned by cultural norms and traditions. Therefore, the expressive function of the source text must be interpreted in light of the source culture and the translator should intervene should such function be misinterpreted or lost in the target text.

The appellative function involves the appeal directed at the receiver's sensitivity, previous experience or disposition to act. Its chief sub-functions include "illustrative, persuasive, imperative, pedagogical, advertising, etc." (Nord, 2009).

Unlike the expressive function, the appellative function is receiver-oriented. The appellative function of a target text is bound to differ from that of the source text because the intended receivers of the two types of texts are different. "This means that the appellative function will not work if the receiver cannot cooperate" (Nord, 2009).

The phatic function aims at establishing/maintaining/ending (social) contact between sender and receiver and its main sub-functions include small talk, taking leave, introductory "peg" for text opening etc. (Nord, 2009).

This function relies on the conventionality of the linguistic, non-linguistic and paralinguistic means used in a particular situation, such as small talk about the weather or the conventional proverb (Nord, 2001a: 44). Therefore, should there be divergence between the source culture and target culture in terms of conventionality, problem will ensue: The phatic function of the source text may be interpreted as referential, expressive or even appellative in the target culture.

4.1.4.2 A Functional Typology of Translation: Documentary Translation and Instrumental Translation

Based on the function of the target text, translation strategies are divided into two types, namely, documentary translation and instrumental translation (Nord, 2001a: 47).

Documentary translation "aims at producing in the target language a kind of document of (certain aspects of) a communicative interaction in which a source-culture sender communicates with a source-culture audience via the source text under source-culture conditions. While instrumental translation aims at producing in the target language an *instrument* for a new communicative interaction between the source-culture sender and a target-culture audience, using (certain aspects of) the source text as a model" (Nord, 2001a: 47).

4.1.4.2.1 Documentary Translation

The target produced through the documentary translation is a text whose main function is metatextual, a sub-function of the referential function. Such a target text is a text about a text, or a text about one or more particular aspects of a text. There are various forms of documentary translation, including interlineal translation (word-for-word translation), literal translation, philological translation, exoticizing translation all focusing on different aspects of the source text (Nord, 2001a: 46).

The subdivision of documentary translation may be shown by Table 1 as below:

Table 1 Documentary Translations (Nord, 2001a: 48)

Functions of translation	document of source-culture communicative interaction for target-culture readership			
Function of target text	metatextual function			
Type of translation	documentary translation			
Form of translation	interlineal translation	literal translation	philological translation	exoticizing translation
Purpose of translation	reproduction of SL* system	reproduction of SL form	reproduction of ST** form + content	reproduction of ST form, content + situation
Focus of translation process	structures of SL lexis + syntax	lexical units of source text	syntactical units of source text	textual units of source text

(continued)

Example	comparative linguistics	quotations in news texts	Greek and Latin classics	modern literary prose

Notes: * SL stands for source language, hereinafter the same.
** ST stands for source text, hereinafter the same.

4.1.4.2.2 Instrumental Translation

The other type of translation under the typological model of Nord is instrumental translation. According to Nord (2001: 50), "the result of an instrumental translation is a text that may achieve the same range of functions as an original text." Instrumental translation may be further divided into equifunctional translation, heterofunctional translation and homologous translation. The subdivision of instrumental translation may be shown by Table 2 as below:

Table 2 Instrumental Translations (Nord, 2001a: 51)

Function of translation	Instrument for target-culture communicative interaction modeled according to source-culture communicative interaction		
Function of target text	referential/expressive/appellative/phatic function and/or sub-functions		
Type of translation	instrumental translation		
Form of translation	equifunctional translation	heterofunctional translation	homologous translation
Purpose of translation	achieve ST function for target audience	achieve similar functions as ST	achieve homologous effect to ST
Focus of translation	functional units of ST	transferable functions of ST	degree of ST originality
Example	instruction for use	*Gulliver's Travels* for children	poetry translated by poet

4.1.4.3 Norms and Conventions in Functional Translation

So far, we have been discussing functional translation from a mostly strategic perspective, i. e., the role of the translation brief, the typology of texts and the selection of the appropriate translation strategy based on the translation brief. In this part, we will look into matters on the operational level of functional translation: norms and convention in translation, which govern the use of verbal and nonverbal signs in a particular text or text type and provide important guidance to the translator in making translation decisions.

According to Nord (2001: 53 – 58), there are four types of conventions at work in functional translation, namely, genre conventions, general style conventions, translation conventions and conventions of nonverbal behavior. In the book, the focus will be on the first three of the four types of convention given the fact that study on the last type of conventions is still in its infancy and that the present book is primarily concerned with translation, as opposed to interpretation.

4. 1. 4. 3. 1 Genre Conventions

Genre conventions come into being as a result of the standardization of communication practices. "As certain kinds of text are used repeatedly in certain situations with more or less the same function or functions, these texts acquire conventional forms that are sometimes raised to the status of social norms" (Nord, 2001a: 53). Genre conventions and norms play a critical role in both text production and text reception because on the one hand, the authors of texts have to comply with the target culture conventions if they want to carry out their communicative intentions and on the other hand text receivers have to rely on the conventional form of the source text to infer the source text producer's intentions (Nord, 2001a: 53).

In view of this, if a target text is to be acceptable as representative of a target-culture genre, the translator must be familiar with and compare the genre conventions of both the source text and the target text (as implied by the translation Skopos), so that he or she will identify the need for adaptations in the translational process and the target text will be acceptable in the target culture (Nord, 2001a: 54).

4. 1. 4. 3. 2 General Style Conventions

General style conventions are another type of conventions that play a role in functional translation. Even when there are similar structures in the two languages involved in the translational process, there is often a difference between them in usage of such structure due to different literary traditions and conventions concerning what are considered good style (Nord, 2001a: 55).

4. 1. 4. 3. 3 Translation Conventions

Translation conventions come into existence because translation in itself is a kind of communication. Translation conventions may be further divided into two sub-types, constitutive translational conventions and regulative translational conventions. The former refer to "the general concept of what a translation is or should be and what kind of relationship is expected to hold between a particular kind of source text and the corresponding target text in translation" (Nord, 2001a: 58), while the latter refers to the procedure used for the handling of particular translation problems below the text rank (for example, proper names, culture-bound realities or quotations) (Nord, 2001a: 55).

4.1.4.4 A Functional Approach to Solving Translation Problems

Another component of German functionalism that may be used to tackle operational-level issues in translation and thereby achieve translation adequacy is the systematic approach to translation problems.

Translation problems refer to problems which have to be solved by the translator in the translation process in order to produce a functionally adequate target text. They are to be differentiated from two other terms: translation difficulties and translation errors. Translation difficulties are which arise due to the translator's deficiency in linguistic, cultural or translational competence or his or her lack of documentation faced by specific translators (Nord, 2001a: 64, 141). Translation problems are objective (or at least intersubjective) while translation difficulties are subjective. Translation errors refer to failures to carry out the instructions implied in the translation brief and as inadequate solutions to translation problems (Nord, 2001a: 75).

Translation problems are divided into four categories, namely, pragmatic problems, cultural problems, linguistic problems and text specific problems, and translation difficulties and translation errors may also be divided along the same line (Nord, 2001a: 64).

Pragmatic translation problems arise as a result of differences between source-text and target-text situations and may be identified by checking on the extra-textual factors (sender, receiver, medium, time, place, motive, text function). Pragmatic translation problems are present in every translation task and are viewed as the most important problems in the translation process in German functionalism (Nord, 2001a: 65).

Cultural translation problems are caused by differences between the source culture and target culture in terms of norms and conventions guiding verbal and non-verbal behaviors in the two cultures. They refer to all the kinds of conventions mentioned in the previous section on translation conventions and norms (Nord, 2001a: 66).

Linguistic translation problems are those arising from structural differences between the source language and target language in terms of vocabulary, syntax and super-segmental features (Nord, 2001a: 66).

Some translation problems are specifically confined to one particular source text, such as certain figures of speech, neologisms or puns. As its definition suggestions, solutions to these text-specific problems cannot be generalized and applied to similar cases, the translator therefore must be prepared to act creatively (Nord, 2001a: 67).

According to traditional approaches to translation, translating is viewed as a code-switching operation in which lexical or syntactic equivalences are crucial, and the translation process works from the linguistic text-surface structures to conventions, and finally to pragmatics. Translators adopting this bottom-up approach tend to stick with the source-text structures and therefore ignore the textual functions in the communication situation often, thus leading to translation errors even if they are translating into their native language (Nord, 2001a: 67).

In view of the deficiency of the bottom-up approach, the German functionalists advocate an alternative approach: Translation problems should be dealt with in a top-down way: The translation process should start on the pragmatic level by deciding on the intended function of the translation (documentary or instrumental). A distinction is then made between those functional elements of the source text that will have to be reproduced "as such" and the ones that must be adapted to the addressee's background knowledge, expectations and communicative needs or to such factors as medium restrictions and deixis requirements. The translation type chosen this way then determines whether the translated text should conform to source-culture or target culture conventions (on the cultural level). Finally, problems posed by differences between the source language and target language are to be solved (Nord, 2001a: 68).

4.1.5 Looking for Help in the Translation Process: The Role of Auxiliary Texts in Solving Translation Problems

So far, the most important view points of the German functionalist approach to translation have been introduced. However, this approach, in its present form, remains vague in some aspects. For example, on the pragmatic level, the translator is supported to make adjustment to the implicit and explicit information in the source text in light of the differences between the source text addressees and target text addressees in terms of source-text-specific information. (Nord, 2001a: 63) While this suggestion provides precious insight for the translator, it does not tell the translator how to find out the "quantity and quality of source-culture-specific knowledge that can be presupposed in the addressed target audience" (Nord, 2007a). Similarly, the functional approach cautions that if the instrumental translation strategy is adopted, the target text must conform to the "conventions of the language use and style (e. g. genre conventions, measurement conventions, conventions of "good style") of the target culture, without clarifying how to identify such conventions and bring the target text in line with them. In response to this, more details need to be added to the functional approach to make it more effective in assisting the translator to complete the translational action and achieve translation adequacy.

According to Nord (2007), the above mentioned difficulties that the translator may encounter with regard to pragmatic, cultural and linguistic information and with regard to translation methods and procedures can be solved with the help of auxiliary texts. As are defined in Section 1. 2. 6 of the book, auxiliary texts may be classified into three types, namely, previous translations, background texts and parallel texts. In the following four sections, the roles that the three types of texts play in the translation process will be discussed.

4.1.5.1 Previous Translations

A previous translation is an existing translation of a particular text. As the rendering by another translator, a previous translation may provide inspiring information to the translator as to the methodology of translation (Nord, 2007a), especially if feedback on the previous translation may be obtained by the new translator, so that he or she may modify his own translation methodology in light of the experiences and lessons offered by such existing translated version of the text.

4.1.5.2 Background Texts

Background texts are valuable to the translator in the following two ways:

First, they are a rich mine of "factual or domain knowledge (with the corresponding conceptualizations and terminology), world and cultural knowledge, and the presuppositions regarding recent developments of the topic in question" (Nord, 2007a).

Second, they are highly useful in tackling the issue of the quantity and quality of the target text addressees' presupposed information about the source text. Background texts, being texts written by target-culture authors for target-readers, contain references to the source-culture.

4.1.5.3 Parallel Texts

Parallel texts are texts on comparable topics, which, despite being produced in differing environments, belong to the same genre and fulfill the same function (House, 2007). When translating a particular text, the translator may consult parallel texts of the text being translated, so as to identify and follow "conventions of language use and style (e. g. genre conventions, measurement conventions, conventions of 'good style')" (Nord, 2007a) and obtain linguistic information, i. e., "system-related specificities (e. g., collocations, idioms and phraseology)". Sometimes, in very standardized genres, a parallel text may even offer the translator with ready-made segments for the translation of the source text. In this case, such parallel text may be used as a model text for translation.

4.2 Applicability and Relevance of German Functionalism to the Present Research

As has been noted at the beginning of this chapter, the German functionalism is adopted as the cornerstone of the theoretical framework of the present book, because this approach to translation practice and studies agrees with the principles and rules drawn up by several generations of Chinese translators, journalists, editors, administrators and other people involved in the international communication of China. In other words, this approach is fully capable of withstanding the tests of translation practice in the context of China's international communication.

It has been pointed out in the first chapter that translation for the international communication of China (including its legal system, of course) is highly purposeful: It is oriented to and proceeds from presenting China to the intended audience (both inside and outside China) in a balanced and truthful way so as to promote the understanding of China by the rest of the world, neutralize the adverse effects of negative coverage of China by the Western media and hence improve the image of China. The target text's primary function is the informative function. In view of this, the instrumental translation strategy should be adopted as the appropriate translation strategy, the target text should conform to the norms and conventions of the target culture, and a receiver-centered approach must be followed so as to solve pragmatic and other translation problems. Such an approach is in perfect concordance with the existing rules and regulations that have been upheld in the translation practice in the international communication of China.

Firstly, "Three In-line-with Principles" for China's International Communication, which are the strategic guidelines for China's international communication and are sanctioned by the government, the initiator of translation, and generally upheld by practitioners and researcher alike, concords with the abovementioned German functionalist approach to translation for the international communication of China. The second of the three principles, namely, the content of such efforts must be in line with the targeted audience's need for information on China, implies that the information in the source text may be adjusted to meet the needs of the audiences, i. e. , text receivers. This principle is supported by the functionalist definition of translation as text-processing action (referred to 4. 1. 1. 6). The third principle, namely, translated texts used for China's international communication must be in line with the norms and conventions in the culture of such targeted language (English, in the context of the book) to ensure that such external publicity efforts of China will achieve their intended effect, fits in perfectly with the functionalist identification of translation for the international communication of China as instrumental translation.

In addition, the first two principles suggest that for the translation to be effective (i. e. , achieve the intended purpose), the translator should decide on what information to transfer (and what not to) and what translation strategy to adopt in light of the need of the intended receiver of the target texts, which conforms to the Skopos rule of functional translation; the last of the three principles, namely, the target text must comply with the norms and conventions, or at least be comprehensible to the target text receivers, fits perfectly with the coherence rule of functional translation and the designation of the Chinese to English translation for international communication as instrumental translation.

Secondly, the rules drawn up by veteran practitioners agree with and are supported by German functionalism. A case in point is the classification of translation errors and the interpretive translation rule proposed by Duan Liancheng (1990), who, on the basis of "more than forty years' experience as a translator" (Duan Liancheng, 1990), divides translation errors in Chinese to English translation in the context of China's international communication into two types. Type-A errors refer to spelling errors, misuse of words and grammatical errors, which are equal to the category of linguistic translation errors in the functional approach. Type-B errors are more complex and are divided into four sub-types.

The first three sub-types are essentially failures to provide presupposed information to the target readers and therefore correspond to the pragmatic translation errors in the functional approach and the remaining type of errors refers to failures to conform to target cultural conventions and norms, which are essentially identical with cultural translation errors in the functional approach. Furthermore, Mr. Duan's "prescriptions" for curing such errors, namely, "interpretive translation", which involves pre-translation processing on the basis of proper comparison between the source and target texts, source-text and target-text receivers also comply with the functionalist approach.

Another case in point is the translation rules drawn up by Shen Suru, another well-respected expert in the field of the international publicity of China. Such translation rules are rendered in plain language and are perfect examples of the tactics that translators adopt in the functionalist instrumental translation: "be aware of the differences between the domestic communication and international communication and keep away from the principles and practices that apply to domestic communication only; make sure that your reporting is readily comprehensible by the intended audience; do necessary modification to the original texts in the translation process, including adding necessary interpretations for culture-loaded matters and leaving out information that is not relevant to the theme of the reporting; be concise, direct and plain in style and avoid loading your writing with florid and fancy but empty phrases." (For more please refer to Section 3.2.2)

Thirdly, German functionalism has already been used to review and guide translation practices in the context of China's international communication and its viability as theoretical support for such practices has been established (范勇, 2009: 6; 张美芳, 2004: 192).

All in all, it can be inferred from the above that the German functionalism is in line with the rules and principles drawn up and followed by practitioners of China's international communication, and can therefore be assumed to have been tested by and applicable to both the practice and study of Chinese to English translation for the international communication of China, including its legal system.

4.3 Summary of This Chapter

In this chapter, the German functionalist approach to translation is introduced and its applicability to the Chinese to English translation for the international communication of China has been confirmed on the ground that this approach echoes with the rules and principles of translation in the context of such international communication and provides a viable for interpreting and guiding such translation. In the following two chapters of the book, the Chinese to English translation of soft legal texts in the context of the international communication of China's legal system will be reviewed, the appropriate translation strategy will be identified and solutions for translation problems will be proposed within the framework of the German functionalist approach to translation.

Chapter Five Chinese to English Translation of Soft Legal Texts in the Context of the International Communication of China: Translation Strategies, Problems and Solutions

In the previous chapter, it is confirmed that the German functional approach to translation is in perfect concordance with the rules and principles that generations of Chinese translators, journalists, administrators and other people involved in the international publicity efforts of China, and hence is adopted as the theoretical foundation of the present research into the Chinese to English legal text translation related to such publicity. In the present chapter, such Chinese to English translation will be analyzed according to the German functional approach, and on the basis of such analysis, the translation strategy and translation problems and solutions will be identified.

5.1 Identifying the Appropriate Translation Strategy

As has been pointed out in section 4.1.4.1, the most appropriate translation strategy for a specific translational action is determined by the intended function of the target language text and on the basis of a proper comparison of the source language text and target language text according to the parameters listed in the translation brief, namely, the intended text function(s), the addressee(s), the (prospective) time and place of text reception, the medium over which the text will be transmitted, and possibly the motive for the production or reception of the text. Identifying the translation brief, which in essence is a detailed breakdown of the translation Skopos or purpose plays a crucial role.

As has been pointed out in chapter one herein, the purpose of China's international communication efforts is to provide the addressees with information on China's legal system, so as to dispel misperception of China's legal system and create a "favorable international environment" for the development of China.

The rules and principles formed on the basis of the experiences of generations of translators and journalists call for "an interpretative translation approach", compliance with the receiver-centered "Three In-line-with Principles"; perhaps most significantly, the Chinese government, which is the ultimate client and initiator of translation for international communication, has stressed on many occasions that texts in the target language "must be natural and readily comprehensible to the addressees" and that the external publicity practitioners, the translators included, "should let facts speak for themselves and refrain from forcing the opinions of China on the addressees" (李长春, 2004; 温家宝, 2007). All these facts point in one direction—the function of target texts in the translation for the international communication of China, its legal system included, is primarily informative and secondarily appellative, and therefore the typical Chinese to English translation for the purpose of introducing China's legal system to the outside world should be classified as instrumental translation and the target texts produced should conform to the norms and conventions of the target culture.

Selecting the instrumental translation for the international communication of China's legal system is commonsensical in that no translation initiator would intend the target text to fulfill the functions of documentary translation, the opposite of instrumental translation, i. e., the metatextual function, or creating a text of text, because as Mr. Shen Suru put it, "the overseas audience are not ready or willing to read or listen to texts that are full of translationese. What they want is idiomatic texts written in their mother tongues and catering to their taste both in terms of contents and form" [外国受众不准备也不愿意阅读或收听"翻译稿件", 他们要看或要听的是地道的外文——内容和形式都十分适合他们的外文 (沈苏儒, 1990: 224)].

This assumption then serves as a starting point of the present section as well as the two following sections, as the function type of translation also determines whether the target texts should follow the cultural norms and conventions and linguistic rules of the source culture or those of the target culture. In the following three parts, the three types of translation problems will be analyzed respectively.

5.2 Translation Problems in the International Communication of China's Legal System: An Analysis According to the Functionalist Approach

The present section is based on the following model: Translation problems in the international communication of the Chinese legal system are first analyzed in the top-down way proposed by the German functional approach, i. e., in the order of pragmatic translation problems, cultural translation problems, and linguistic translation problems, so as to find out the contributing factors to such problems.

5.2.1 Pragmatic Translation Problems in the International Communication of China's Legal System: Contributing Factors and Solutions

According to the top-down functional approach to solving translation problems, the first thing to do is to identify the translation function, which in turn, is determined by the intended communicative function(s) of the target text, not the source text (Nord, 2001a: 39). Now that the translation type and target text function(s) have been identified in the previous section, the translator should then proceed to "compare the profiles of the source and target texts according to the translation brief" (Nord, 2009), because such comparison between the source-text and the target-text profiles will provide a clear picture of what source-text information or linguistic elements may be kept invariant in the target text and what has to be adjusted to the requirements of the translation purpose (Nord, 2001a: 64), because pragmatic translation problems arise as a result of differences between source-text and target-text situations and may be identified by examining such extra-textual factors as the sender, receiver, medium, time, place, motive and text function, which correspond with the components of the translation brief. In view of this, the next step to solve pragmatic translation problems is to compare the source text and target text according to the components of the translation brief, which should be provided as much detailed information as possible.

5.2.1.1 Comparison of the Intended Functions between Source Text and Target Text

As has been pointed out in section 5. 1, the target text in the international communication is primarily produced to serve the translation Skopos, i. e. , providing genuine information on the Chinese legal system and thereby neutralize the misperception of China's legal system. Therefore, the target text has two functions, namely, informative function and appellative function, with the former taking precedence over the latter.

The source text, however, is more complex. Take the average source text—media reports on China's legal system (either as a whole or any specific aspect of it such as legislation, enforcement, administration of justice, etc.) for example. Although there has been a consensus in China that the outdated, propaganda-oriented approach must be replaced with a new information-oriented approach based on modern journalism and communication theories, many news media in China, especially those run or sponsored by the government, still resort from time to time to tactics reminiscent of the discredited old approach, such as empty-sounding clichés, grandiose style of writing, rigid officialese and bureaucracy, viewing themselves as part of the bureaucratic apparatus instead of news medias (罗建华, 2007). As a result, many news reports carried by Chinese media tend to be more appellative and/or expressive in function than their parallel texts in the Western media (罗建华, 2007), although they are nonetheless also primarily informative in function. Therefore, the expressive and appellative functions of such source text must be reduced or even neutralized by removing or "toning down" markers of such functions so that the translation Skopos will be realized and the requirements of the translation brief will be met. In this case, hetero-functional translation, a sub-type of instrumental translation should be the optimal translation strategy. In other cases, where the functions of the source text and the target text are the same or identical, another sub-type of instrumental translation, namely, equi-functional translation should be adopted, according to which the function markers in the source text should be preserved in the target text.

5.2.1.2 Comparison of the Addressees between Source Text and Target Text

According to the German functionalist approach, comparison between the intended receiver of the source text and that of the target is made primarily for the purpose of identifying their difference in cultural knowledge, because such disparity between the two sides "may require an adjustment of the relationship between explicit and implicit information in the text" (Nord, 2001a: 63). In other words, if any of the implicit information in the source text that the source text producer can reasonably assume to be in the possession of the source text addressee is, however, beyond the knowledge of the addressee of the target text, such information must be made explicit to the target text addressee. In this view, it may also be inferred that information in the source text that is not interesting, useful or otherwise not necessary to the target text addressee, or information that may even undermine the very purpose of translation should either be left out or made implicit, just as the late Duan Liancheng, a veteran journalist and translator, argued more than two decades ago (段连城, 1990).

As to the content and extent of the typical addressee of source text and his or her counterpart in the target culture, it can be assumed that the latter knows very little about China. Since academic literature on cultural differences between China and the English-speaking world is abundant, the present research then leaves this issue as such.

However, a few more words must be said about the differences between the Chinese legal system and the legal system(s) of the jurisdiction where the target text addressee is from. In the present research, the English translations of the source texts are primarily intended for Anglophone countries of the world, which are mostly former British colonies and hence inherited the common law system, a legal system first came into existence in Great Britain. While the source text addressee is from China, whose legal system is based on the civil law system, and is influenced by the Confucian tradition.

Although both the legal system of China and that of Anglophone countries like the United States may be divided into three branches, namely the legislative branch (responsible for making laws), the judicial branch (responsible for administering laws) and the enforcement branch (responsible for enforcing laws), there are some remarkable differences between the two systems:

Firstly, the source of law, i. e., what may be counted as law. In a legal system based on the common law tradition, the primary source of law is judgments, or precedents, as they are formally known. It can be said that common law is essentially judge-made case law, in which binding precedents may be used in hearing new cases. On the other hand, the source of law of a legal system based on the civil law tradition is codified laws, "which derive from a legislative process and which courts have to consider in their judgments as well and beside existing judge-made precedents" (Lengeling, 2008).

Secondly, the role of precedents. Judges in a legal system based on common law, previous court decisions are analyzed to find a general principle in each of them and apply such principle to solve new disputes; while civil law judges are primarily bound to statutes and reason (Lengeling, 2008).

Thirdly, method of legal thinking and finding justice. This is the true difference between common law and civil law. In common law, the judge focuses on each single case and plays the central role. In contrast, the judge's role is to apply abstract principles developed regardless of single cases.

Fourthly, appointment and selection of judges. In a common-law-based legal system, judges are selected from experienced and successful practicing lawyers while judges in a civil law system is appointed and are not required to have experiences as practicing lawyers.

To sum up, The legal system of China is vastly different from those of Anglophone countries. As a result, the source culture and target culture are bound to differ considerably from each other in terms of legal terminology, i. e., words and expressions denoting legal concepts and institutions. In view of this, the following principles must be followed to facilitate the understanding by the target text addressee of source culture legal terminology: The legal institutions and concepts in the source culture should be translated into their counterpart institutions and concepts in the target culture whenever possible. However, if there are no such counterparts, new terms may be coined in accordance with rules applicable to legal system of the target culture, and interpretation may be made to such coinages whenever possible (杜金榜, 2005).

5.2.1.3 Comparison of the Medium, Time and Place between Source Text and Target Text

In this part, three factors, namely, the medium or media through which the texts and the time and place that such texts are made are brought under the same heading for discussion in consideration of the technical nature thereof.

According to the German functionalism, communicative interactions take place in situations that are limited in time and space. This means every situation has historical and cultural dimensions that condition the agents' verbal and nonverbal behavior, their knowledge and expectations of each other, their appraisal of the situation, and the standpoint from which they look at the world. Therefore, should differences in time and space may affect the realization of the translation Skopos, the translator must make necessary adjustments. For example, if the source text and target text are received in different years, different temporal deixis may be needed in the target text so as to remind the target text receiver of such difference in time (Nord, 2001a: 63).

The factor of medium or media is the same case. If difference in the medium through which the texts are transmitted affects the transfer of information and thereby may undermine the realization of translation Skopos, the translator must make necessary adjustments in the translation process. For example, when the target is released in print form and the space set for such text is not enough because the target text is expanded to accommodate the addressee' lack of source-culture knowledge, downsizing of the text will then be necessary and in this case, the least important function of the text might have to be sacrificed (Nord, 2001a: 63).

To sum up, in the context of the Chinese to English translation of soft legal texts in the context of international communication of China's legal system, the way to uncover and solve pragmatic translation problems is identifying the optimal translation strategy on the basis of a thorough analysis of the profiles of both the source text and target text and adopting proper translation strategies.

5. 2. 2 Cultural Translation Problems in the International Communication of China's Legal System: Contributing Factors and Solutions

Cultural translation problems are caused by differences between the source culture and target culture in terms of norms and conventions guiding verbal and nonverbal behaviors in the two cultures involved in the translation process. As it has been confirmed in the previous section that the Chinese to English translation of soft legal texts in the context of international communication of China's legal system should be instrumental translation, translation problems in this category in the context of China's efforts to introduce its legal system to the rest of the world then arise as a result of the failure of the target text to fully conform to target cultural conventions and norms, including genre conventions, general style conventions, translation conventions and conventions of nonverbal behavior.

The key to solving the cultural translation problems, then, lies in identifying the differences of the target culture conventions and norms concerning the target text. Like in the previous section, the typical soft legal texts, namely law-themed media reports are again adopted as examples.

Generally speaking, a typical English journalistic text (to be more specific, a hard English journalistic text) conforms to the following conventions and norms.

In terms of structure, a typical journalistic text consists of a title (sometimes made up of a main title and a subtitle), a lead, and a main body. The title is in essence a condensation of the journalistic text, while the lead is the first paragraph or first sentence of the text, which presents the reader with the latest, most important or most interesting information of the text, usually covering the five Ws and an H—who, what, when, where, why and how, i. e., the most newsworthy information in the text (王丽, 2010). The lead and the main body of the text form an inverted pyramid structure in terms of information layout, like "a simple triangle with one side drawn horizontally at the top and the body pointing down. The widest part at the top represents the most substantial, interesting, and important information the writer means to convey, illustrating that this kind of material should head the article, while the tapering lower portion illustrates that other material should follow in order of diminishing importance"①, as is shown by Figure 2 as below:

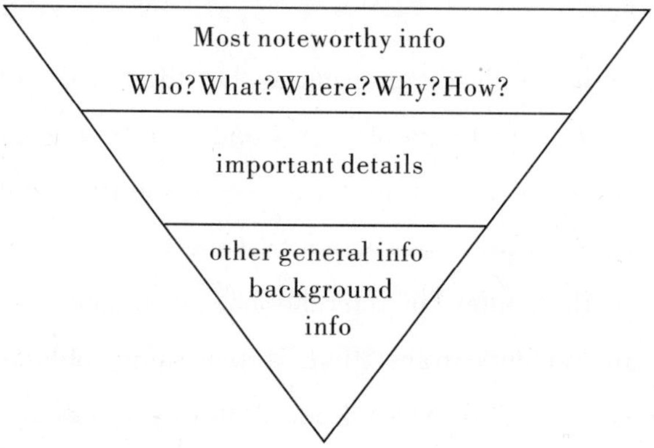

Figure 2② Inverted Triangle Structure of a Typical English Journalistic Text

In terms of style, a typical English journalistic text needs to be intelligible to the majority of readers, as well as to be engaging and succinct in style. Plain yet clear language is preferred (袁晓, 2010). In particular, the headline should be as concise as possible. Short but powerful words, acronyms, abbreviations, and witty coinages are frequently used to capture the attention of potential readers, as is also the case in the main body of the text. Many grammatical components, such as articles, conjunctions, person relative pronouns and auxiliaries, are omitted from the headline whenever possible (张健, 2004: 4 – 5). To save space and enhance the sense of timeliness, simple present, simple future and present continuous are the most frequently used tenses.

In terms of professionalism, objectivity is upheld as somewhat idealized pro-

---

① Retrieved from http://en.wikipedia.org/wiki/Inverted_pyramid.

② Retrieved from http://en.wikipedia.org/wiki/Inverted_pyramid.

fessional standard; misinformation propaganda, distortion and sensationalism are frowned upon. ①

Hence, in the top-down way approach to translation, the information selected (and added) through the pragmatic step of the translation process should then be rendered into English according to the above norms and conventions as appropriate in the target culture, so as to solve the cultural translation problems.

5.2.3 Linguistic Translation Problems in the International Communication of China's Legal System: Contributing Factors and Solutions

If the top-down functional approach to solving translation problems is followed, after the first two steps of the translation process are completed, namely solving the pragmatic and cultural translation problems, it will hardly be necessary to address the difference in language system, because by then a total translation solution will have already been formed, even if there is still more than one possible solution after the first two steps are completed, the optimal solution may either be chosen by contextual aspects or even, in the translators' own personal preferences, provided that the function of the translation (instrumental translation in the case of the present book) is respected (Nord, 2001a: 68).

As a matter of fact, linguistic translation errors, i. e., failure to solve the linguistic translation problems, arise as a result of the traditional bottom-up approaches, in which translating is viewed as a code-switching operation where lexical or syntactic equivalences are crucial, and the translation process works from the linguistic text-surface structures to conventions, and finally to pragmatics. Translators adopting this bottom-up approach tend to stick with the source-text structures and therefore ignore the textual functions in the communication situation often, thus leading to translation errors even if they are translating into their native language.

In view of this, the solution to translation problems on the language level is

① Retrieved from http://en.wikipedia.org/wiki/Inverted_pyramid.

to replace the traditional bottom-up approach to the functional top-down way of dealing with translation problems.

5. 2. 4 A Roadmap to Solving Translation Problems in the International Communication of China's Legal System: The Top-down Functional Approach

So far in this chapter, the translation problems in the translation related to China's efforts to introduce its legal system to the outside world have been discussed within the German functionalist framework and a functionalist top-down approach has been proposed to solve such problems. However, the solution put forward is an overall strategy, and a roadmap, so to speak, for solving translation problems. However, as it takes road signs as well as a road map for a traveler to reach his or her destination, the functionalist top-down approach must be enhanced with practical tactics if it were to be viable, because this approach is still vague in many aspects. For example, on the pragmatic level, this approach advises the translator to make adjustment to the implicit and explicit information in the source text in light of the differences between the source text addressees and target text addressees in terms of source-text-specific information. While this suggestion provides precious insight for the translator and has been proved as necessary by decades of international communication practice of China, it does not tell the translator how to find out the "quantity and quality of source-culture-specific knowledge that can be presupposed in the addressed target audience" (Nord, 2007a).

Similarly, the functionalist top-down approach cautions that in the Chinese to English translation related to China's external publicity, the target text must conform to the "conventions of language use and style (e. g. genre conventions, measurement conventions, conventions of 'good style')" (Nord, 2007a) of the target culture, without saying how to identify such conventions and bring the target text in line with them.

Last but not least, as has been pointed out, the translation of legal terminology plays a crucial role in the translation of both hard and soft legal texts, and that legal terms in the source text should be translated into the corresponding legal terms in the target culture whenever possible and where there is no such counterpart for the source culture legal term, a coinage may be made according to the rules of the target culture. This rule seems clear enough; however, as translators involved in the translation of legal terms would argue (Biel, 2008; Mishchenko, 2009), the translation of legal terms is often a complex frustrating process and the principle put forward here in the functional approach needs further details. In response to this, more details will be added to the functional approach to make more practical.

According to Nord (2007), the above mentioned difficulties that the translator may encounter with regard to pragmatic, cultural and linguistic information and with regard to translation methods and procedures, may be solved with the help of auxiliary texts.

5.2.5 Solving Translation Problems with the Help of Auxiliary Texts

Depending on the problems and difficulties that they may help to solve, auxiliary texts may be classified into three types, namely, previous translations, background texts and parallel texts (Nord, 2007). In the following parts of this section, the roles that the three types of texts play in facilitating the translation process will be discussed.

5.2.5.1 Previous Translations as Source of Translation-related Methodological Information: Translation of *Digong An* (《狄公案》)

Previous translations (of the same or a similar text) may provide the translators with methodological information. Translation problems have been solved during the past 2000 years or more. Therefore, most problems a translator comes across in a particular translation task today have already been solved one way or another before (Nord, 2007). The success or failure of such previous translations may provide the translator with important information on translation methodology.

In the context of the Chinese to English translation of soft legal texts for the international communication of China's legal system, a case in point is the *Celebrated Cases of Judge Dee* (*Digong An*), the English translation by Robert Van Gulik (高罗佩), a Dutch diplomat and prominent Sinologist, of *Digong An*, a 18th century Chinese detective novel about the exploits of Di Renjie (Judge Dee), a Tang Dynasty politician. *Celebrated Cases of Judge Dee* is the first ever full English translation of a traditional Chinese detective novel (公案小说). This translation, together with subsequent Judge novels that Gulik wrote in English, not only established the image of Judge Dee (狄仁杰) as an oriental Sherlock Holmes, but also provides precious insight into the traditional Chinese legal system. Today, this translation remains a popular novel as well as a must-read book for scholars of the history, law and society of China (cf. footnotes 10 and 11 to the present book). In this sense, *Celebrated Cases of Judge Dee* is a success story in introducing China's legal system in a more subtle way (张萍, 2007: 110 - 111).

For a translator who is commissioned to translate a similar text, i. e., a law-themed literary work, the methodology adopted by Gulik will be highly valued, as is underscored by the persistent popularity of the translation.

The approach adopted by Gulik may be cited as a classic case of German functionalism, although by the time when he passed away in 1967, the German functionalism as a school of translation studies had not come into existence. Following are some of most important features of Gulik translation methodology.

First, a high sense of translation Skopos. Gulik, as an ardent lover of the Chinese culture, decided to translate *Digong An*, because he felt that traditional Chinese detective novels, being a well-developed genre, should be given its due place in the world (Gulik, 1976: I), and that the traditional Chinese legal system, in spite of the misperception by the West, actually "worked well" for hundreds of years and did have its merits, a claim supported by Sir George Staunton, who was the translator of the *Great Qing Code* (《大清律例》). All translation decisions of Gulik were made according to this Skopos, including the very decision to translate *Digong An* (this novel is the closest among its kind to its Western counterparts, and is sophisticated in plot and hence appeals to the reader).

Second, a keen awareness of the reader. Gulik made it clear that the translated book is for "the general reader" (Gulik, 1976: 227) and kept in mind of the differences between the intended reader of the translation and readers of the Chinese original in terms of their knowledge of "peculiar Chinese situations", time and place (Gulik, 1976: 229). Therefore, he adopted a reader-centered stance when processing the information in the source text, eliminating information that is not necessary to follow the story and may instead confuse the reader, and interpolated an occasional explanatory sentence in the text, providing detailed background information in the preface and appendix of the book, and adopting existing English counterparts of Chinese legal and cultural terms whenever possible, all of which tactics would have been acclaimed by German functionalists. All in all, he actually followed a more instrumental translation strategy, in spite of his claim that the translation is "on the whole a literal one".

To sum up, the success of *Celebrated Cases of Judge Dee* owes to the considerate and flexible approach adopted by the translator, who viewed the original text as an offer of information that he could adjust in light of the need of the readers and ultimately the translation Skopos, and accordingly deployed a wide range of to-the-point coping tactics that not only preserved the spirit of the original text but also enhanced the readability of the target language text.

5.2.5.2 Background Texts as a Source of Pragmatic Information: Translation of "严打"

Background texts are useful in helping the translator solve translation problem in that first they provide the translator with information that otherwise is not available in the source text; second, they help the translator assess the target text addressees' presupposed information about the source text, which is not only crucial in deciding on adjusting the explicit and implicit information in the source text. In this way, the translator can avoid two pragmatic translation errors: Failure to provide sufficient background information to the target reader (or failure to provide such information at all) and providing such information by lengthy notes which spoils the fun of reading.

For example, when a translator is commissioned to translate a soft legal text on "strike-hard" (严打) into English, he may find the following excerpt from the description of a book titled "*Strike Hard! Anti-Crime Campaigns and Chinese Criminal Justice*, 1979 – 1985"① quite useful in that it not only provides him with both the literal translation and more idiomatic translation of the term "严打", namely, "strike hard" and "anti-crime campaign", but also provides him with information on the origin of such campaigns.

As it set forth to achieve rapid modernizing economic growth under the leadership of Deng Xiaoping, the People's Republic simultaneously undertook to reform China's criminal justice system in order to make it more efficient, more accountable to central authority, and better suited to the task of maintaining public order in a changing economic and social environment. Taking a historical approach, this book draws on a wide variety of openly and internally published laws, legal interpretations, talks, speeches, Communist Party documents, collections of criminal cases and other sources ranging from the 1950s to the 1990s in order to portray the development of the Chinese criminal justice system between 1979 and 1985 and to place these changes in the context of the reform agenda of Deng's China. Particular attention is paid to the practice of criminal justice and the reform of prisoners, to the role of campaigns in the development of the Chinese criminal justice system, and to the relationship between crime trends, criminal justice and modernization.

And by reading the following further report by BBC, the translator would notice that the parts in bold and underlined are in fact translations of "严打", and infer that explanation made to the reader regarding the Chinese notion "严打" may be done by adding the phrase "anti-crime campaign" to the literal, word-for-word translation of the Chinese word, as is shown by the first of the underlined part in the news report below:

① http://www.uhpress.hawaii.edu/p-6796-9781885445049.aspx.

China executes notorious gang.

China has executed 14 members of a criminal gang accused of committing the bloodiest crime spree in the country's recent history.

China has hailed the capture of the gang as a victory for its current "strike hard" anti-crime campaign.

Gang leader Zhang Jun was found guilty of leading his accomplices in a series of violent robberies at banks and jewellery stores which left twenty-eight people dead over a period of almost 10 years.

The executions come as China is in the midst of a major anti-crime drive which has led to at least 500 executions in recent weeks for crimes ranging from murder to robbery and embezzlement.

Zhang Jun, 34, was executed in the south-western city of Chongqing, scene of a bungled bank robbery last year which finally led to his capture.

China's official news agency said his leading ally, Li Zejun, and 12 other gang members were also put to death.

They included four women, all of whom claimed to be lovers of the gang leader.

Their sentencing last month was carried live on state television and Chinese newspapers have reported how Zhang Jun forced several of his lovers and friends to carry out murders at random purely in order to bind them further into his web of crime.

China has launched a major anti-crime drive.

On at least three occasions he hired migrant workers at local labour markets, then drove out into the hills and forced his friends to shoot them dead.

China has hailed the capture of the gang as a victory for its current "strike hard" anti-crime campaign, yet some state newspapers have asked why it took so long to bring the gang members to justice.

Foreign human rights groups have warned that the tough campaign may on some occasions have led to the death penalty being handed down for crimes which otherwise would lead only to a jail sentence.

5.2.5.3 Parallel Texts as a Source of Cultural and Linguistic Information

Staying with the translational action mentioned in 5. 2. 5. 2, the BBC report quoted there may also be viewed as a parallel text if the soft legal text that the translator is working on is also a news report. In this case, the parallel text may provide important insights to the translator on the conventions of language use and style (e. g. genre conventions, measurement conventions, conventions of "good style") (Nord, 2007a), such as the information distribution structure as is vividly shown by Figure 4 in the present book, the clear and concise style, etc, and make corresponding adjustments to the translation that he or she produces.

5.2.5.4 Terminology Mining by Auxiliary Texts: "钓鱼执法" "飙车" "人肉搜索" and Many More

Put in a nutshell, terminology mining means to search for a functionally adequate translation(s) of source language terms in auxiliary texts. It consists of three steps: Find online auxiliary texts through search engines, especially Google (this process is also known as googling), identify potential translation(s) of the term in question, search for further auxiliary texts with such translation to verify whether it is correct, in habitual use and unmarked in situations similar to that in which the translation will be used. Proper terminology mining not only enhances the confidence of inverse translators (translators who do not translate into their mother tongue and are therefore more susceptible to source language inferences, including Chinese translators who translate from Chinese into English), but also increases the functionality and naturalness of translation by providing the translators with functionally adequate translations that are otherwise not available in bilingual dictionaries (Biel, 2008).

This approach is highly relevant in the present research, because the Chinese to English translation of soft legal texts in the context of China's international communication is mostly carried out by Chinese translators (as has been noted in Section 2. 2. 2 herein), who are more susceptible to source language inferences and may therefore produce texts containing translationese.

In this part, the translations of the three Chinese words selected from soft legal texts on important judicial events in China in recent years are identified through terminology mining, so as to provide inspirations to translators who are often frustrated by their failure to find functionally adequate translations of terms in existing bilingual dictionaries.

The first of the three Chinese words is renrou sousuo (人肉搜索; literally, human flesh search). This rather unsettling-sounding word was coined by Chinese netizens to refer to the "Internet phenomenon of massive researching using Internet media such as blogs and forums"①. "The name (human flesh search) refers both to the use of knowledge contributed by human beings through social networking, as well as the fact that the searches are usually dedicated to finding the identity of a human being who has committed some sort of offense or social breach online. People conducting such research are commonly referred to collectively as 'Human Flesh Search Engines'."② Because its potential violation of the privacy of individuals, this phenomenon has been the topic of many soft legal texts, i. e., media reports.

The key to find the functionally adequate translation of this term lies in identifying the search key words, which in turn are identified through "educated guess". As Chinese coinages sometimes are translated on a word-by-word basis or even by transliteration by Western media for the sake of giving their stories a sense of exoticism and thereby attract readers (范勇, 2010), an online search is first made with "human flesh search engine" and "China" are the key words. After sifting through the auxiliary texts yielded by the Google search, in which texts produced by respected sources in English-speaking countries should naturally be given priority, the underlined parts in the following text excerpts are identified as candidate translations:

"Human-flesh search engines , such as *renrou sousuo yinqing*, have become a Chinese phenomenon: They are a form of online vigilante justice in which Internet users hunt down and punish people who have attracted their wrath. The goal is to get the targets of a search fired from their jobs, shamed in front of their neigh-

---

① http://en.wikipedia.org/wiki/Human_flesh_search_engine.

② http://en.wikipedia.org/wiki/Human_flesh_search_engine.

bors, run out of town. It's crowd-sourced detective work, pursued online — with offline results."

—*New York Times*, March 3, 2010①

"This is the name given to the Internet-powered manhunts that have achieved notoriety across China this year. A human flesh search engine is where thousands of volunteer cybervigilantes unite to expose the personal details of perceived evildoers and publish them on the Web."

—*Forbes*, November 21, 2008②

Further searches with those candidate translations then establish their credibility as natural and unmarked translation of the Chinese term because they are adopted in a variety of auxiliary texts carried by well-respected mainstream media organizations or academic institutions. The translator, then, may choose from the candidate translations on the basis of a careful comparison of the function of the intended translated text and those of the auxiliary texts.

However, a question arises here: Those translations are retrieved from auxiliary texts written by native-speakers of the English language, then what if the search results are mainly written by non-native speakers of the language, say by journalists of the *China Daily*? This author believes that in this case, the candidate translations by non-native English speakers may be accepted on a tentative basis and be used as part of the search key words so as to verify their credibility or even find better alternatives. Take the translation of the word "钓鱼执法" for example. This term, which describes a form of law enforcement malpractice, did not receive as much attention as "人肉搜索" and English auxiliary texts related to this word are mostly carried by China-based English websites.

In an report carried by *China Daily*, *titled Driver cuts finger to protest "police trap"*③, the notion "钓鱼执法" was rendered into "police trap" "entrapped" and "entrapment". A search with "entrap" "Shanghai" "taxi" and "finger" then yielded more results supporting the viabilities of the translations by

① Retrieved from http://www.nytimes.com/2010/03/07/magazine/07Human-t.html? pagewanted=all.

② Retrieved from http://www.forbes.com/2008/11/21/human-flesh-search-tech-identity08-cx_cb_1121obrien.html.

③ Retrieved from http://www.chinadaily.com.cn/china/2009-10/20/content_8816730.htm.

China Daily, and through a further search with the words "entrap", "police" and "driver" confirmed that the word "entrapment" may be used in similar situations in English-speaking countries, as is testified by an report titled *Police drink-drive "entrapment"*① on *New Zealand Herald* and many other similar texts on websites based in English-speaking countries.

Lastly, what should the translator do if even translations by non-native speakers are not available and the translator has to be the first to translate a Chinese term into English? Even in this case, terminology mining still works and for that matter, works well. Take yet another word, "飙车" for example, which is associated with a hit-and-run traffic accident in 2009 in which a young man was killed by a driver engaged in street racing. By consulting Chinese auxiliary texts, the translator would not only find out more about the incident but also would know that such phenomenon is not confined to China. He could then assume that similar accidents may have occurred somewhere else in the world, and have been reported. With this assumption, the translator could choose "hit-and-run", "high speed", "car" and "killed" as key words. A report on www. canada. com titled *High-speed Street Race Claims Life* would attract his attention; and a further search with "high-speed street race" "crime" "illegal" and "court" as key words would turn up another article *Passenger Killed in High-Speed Race on Riverside Surface Streets*②, in which drag-racing is used as an alternative to high-speed racing. Incidentally, these two words are exactly the most used translations of the term "飙车" in the coverage of the tragic incident in China.

So far, the key roles played by auxiliary texts in helping the translator achieve translation Skopos and realize translation adequacy have been introduced. It can be said that auxiliary texts are valuable resources for the translators in the age of information technology, who are often facing tough deadlines in their daily work. In view of this, ways to find auxiliary texts related to the Chinese to English translation of soft legal texts in a more time-efficient way will be introduced in the following parts of this chapter.

---

① http://www. nzherald. co. nz/nz/news/article. cfm? c_id = 1&objectid = 10733129.

② http://www. nbclosangeles. com/news/local/Passenger-Killed-in-Riverside-Street-Race – 142410645. html.

5.2.6 Finding Auxiliary Texts

Auxiliary texts may either be in print form or electronic form, or in both forms, as long as they are helpful to the translator. For example, the same article on China's legal system may both be carried by a printed version of an academic magazine and stored in the database of an electronic database. However, in the information age when the computer and the Internet are replacing paper and pen as the tools that translators work with, searching online is by far the most convenient—and in most cases, the most economical—means of finding auxiliary texts.

According to the state that such auxiliary texts are in, the auxiliary texts may be classified into two types, namely ready-made auxiliary texts and self-made auxiliary texts.

5.2.6.1 Ready-made Auxiliary Texts

Ready-made auxiliary texts refer to those that have been collected and ready for use, though not always for the purpose of translation. Auxiliary texts of this type are mainly found in large databases, which, however, often charge a fee for access to such texts. Therefore, auxiliary texts of this type may be beyond the reach of some translators. However, if a translator is a member of an institution which is a subscriber to such databases, such as a university, or agovernment agency, etc, the translator may access to the auxiliary texts for free.

The most prominent among such databases include "Heinonline", "Lexis-Nexis", "Westlaw", "Thompson-Reuters" and "Chinalawinfo", among others.

5.2.6.2 Self-made Auxiliary Texts

Auxiliary texts in this category refer to those which the translator has to glean from the Internet by himself. The following types of websites are where it is most likely to find such auxiliary texts:

Websites of the government agencies of English-speaking countries and international organizations where English is the/a working language; for example, translators of the sample source texts quoted in Section 5.2 of the present book may well find many inspiring parallel texts on the website of the Ministry of Justice of the United States; since Chinese and English are both working languages of the United Nations, many UN documents, including those related to law, have a Chinese version and an English version, which are excellent auxiliary texts.

Websites of universities, colleges and other academic institutions. With the rise of China as an important member of the international community, there has been increasing interest in the legal system of China and many academic institutions have set up Chinese law centers or institutions. Many texts on the websites of such centers or institutions are very useful as auxiliary texts, such as this full-length translation of a Chinese law posted on the China Law Center of the University of Yale retrievable at http://www.law.yale.edu/documents/pdf/Intellectual_Life/Ch_China_Adopts_1st_OGI_Regulations.pdf.

Websites of business and industry associations, especially those having an eye on China, such as the website of the Australia China Business Council, which offers regular free newsletters on China, including aspects of the legal system of China.

Websites of business enterprises, such as law firms, accounting firms, etc. For example, Covington & Burling LLP, an international law firm having office in many cities of the world, including Beijing, release information concerning China's legal practice and even translation of Chinese laws via its website.

Websites of newspapers, magazines, and other media from English speaking countries. It is noteworthy that in recent years, some leading newspapers in the English-speaking world have launched English-Chinese bilingual versions, such as http://www.ftchinese.com/, operated by Financial Times, and http://cn.wsj.com/gb/bilingual.asp, which is run by the Wallstreet Journal. Many reports on such bilingual websites appear in both English and Chinese, and two versions may be read side by side.

China-themed websites and weblogs run by foreign nationals who are interested in China. Some of the most influential websites in this category are www. danwei. com, which "started in 2003 as a daily report on the Chinese media and Internet with translations, original articles, videos and blog posts"①, and its mission is to "examine and analyze state and commercial media, social media, and official statements"②. Another prominent example is http://blog. hiddenharmonies. org, which claims that its mission is "to articulate and seek out Chinese perspectives, smart perspectives, and translations of Chinese perspectives from around world. It is run by people who love China. It is about fostering a community of intellectual and influential citizens from around the world interested in China to comment, discuss, praise or critique (as the case may be) a world that is fast-changing."③

A website of this category that is especially valuable for the present book and indeed for the Chinese to English translation for the international communication of China's legal system is http://www. chinalawblog. com/, which is dedicated to "discuss the practical aspects of Chinese law and how it impacts business there" ④and provide many insights into the business laws and regulations of China from a foreigner's perspective.

A collection of the above types of websites prepared by D'Angelo Law Library of the University of Chicago Law School is included as an appendix to the book.

Of course, auxiliary texts can be found by the most fool-proof means of searching with Google, or by "Googling" (Biel, 2008). However, this author has to remind the translators engaged in the Chinese to English translation of soft legal texts in the context of international communication of China's legal system that auxiliary texts found online must be taken with pint of salt, as there may be ideological, economic and/cultural differences between the initiators of translation and the authors of such parallel texts, and therefore and such differences are likely to be manifested in the auxiliary texts.

---

① http://www. danwei. com/about/.

② http://www. danwei. com/about/.

③ http://blog. hiddenharmonies. org.

④ http://www. chinalawblog. com/about/.

5.3 Summary of This Chapter

So far in this chapter, the Chinese to English translation of soft legal texts in the context of the international communication of China's legal system is discussed within the framework of German functionalism and the translation strategy, translation problems and solutions are proposed. In addition, the instrumental role of auxiliary texts in implementing translation strategy and solving translation problems are also discussed in detail on the basis of concrete examples. In the following chapter, translation errors in the international communication of China's legal system will be reviewed and solutions proposed on the basis of the strategy, approach and tactics identified in this chapter.

Chapter Six Addressing Errors in the Chinese to English Translation of Soft Legal Texts for the International Communication of China's Legal System: A Functionalist Approach in Action

In this chapter, examples of genuine translation errors in the international communication of China's legal system will be examined in light of German functionalism, especially the top-down functionalist approach proposed in the previous chapter, and solutions to such errors will be proposed on the basis of such analysis.

Examples used in this chapter are divided into two groups according to their origin, namely, those selected from texts released by specialized international communication entities and those uncovered from target texts released by concurrent international communication entities (as are defined in Section 2. 2. 3 of the book). This classification is made due to the fact that the soft legal texts released by the former categories of entities are either directly written in English or translated into English on the basis of Chinese texts which are unfortunately beyond the reach of the author of the present book while those released by the second group of entities are accessible by the author. The translation errors in the first category are mostly associated with the translation of words and phrases, especially legal and semi-legal terms, while the translation errors in the second group are selected from English translations of whole Chinese texts.

6. 1 Translation Errors in Texts Released by Specialized International Communication Entities of China

Given their roles as long-established agencies dedicated to the international communication of China, specialized international communication entities of China are staffed with well-trained journalists, editors and other professionals, who may also work side by side with foreign experts. As a result, the translation errors identified in the English soft legal texts released by such entities are primarily on the pragmatic and cultural level and rarely involve linguistic translation errors.

6.1.1 Regulations or Regulation?

Following a string of fatal school bus accidents in China, China has stepped up its legislative efforts in school bus safety and a new by-law has been promulgated, namely, *Administrative Regulation on School Bus Security* (《校车安全管理条例》). However, readers of *China Daily* report titled "China adopts school bus safety regulation"① would be confused as to the exact number of regulatory documents released, for although the title of the report suggests only one document is released, the lead of report, "the State Council, China's cabinet, has approved a draft of regulations on school bus safety management, according to a statement issued Thursday", suggests otherwise, as may be inferred from the plural form of the word "regulation".

Furthermore, a report released by www.china.org.cn, another specialized international communication entity, which is titled "*School Bus Regulations Draft Issued*" would also confuse its readers because as the title suggests more than one "regulation" has been passed, the entire report exclusively deals with only one regulatory document. A survey of reports released by other international communication entities of China reveals that similar confusion also exists.

This state of affairs is due to the fact that when it refers to an individual by-law, the word "regulation" is used in its singular form in English-speaking countries like the United States, as may be tested by the terminology mining approach proposed in the previous chapter. However, due to some reason, the plural form of the word is sometimes used in China to refer to a single legislation. This inconsistency may cause misunderstanding in international communication, as is testified by the following report posted on www.schoolbusfleet.com, a Canada-

① Retrieved from http://www.chinadaily.com.cn/china/2012-03/29/content_14946017.htm.

based school bus industry information portal website:

China Approves Bevy of School Bus Regulations

China's State Council approved long-awaited school bus safety regulations on Tuesday, following several fatal crashes in recent months involving "modified and sometimes overcrowded" school buses, China Daily reports.

The regulations, which go into effect immediately, give buses priority in traffic congestion and require companies and drivers to acquire licenses to offer school transportation services. Other drivers are barred from overtaking a bus when students are boarding or disembarking, and school buses must operate on routes mapped out by authorities.

Schools and bus companies have been given a 90-day grace period to comply with the regulations.

It can be inferred from the word "bevy" (which means a group of or a host of) and the missing article "a" before the phrase "long-awaited school bus safety regulations" in the first sentence of the report that the author actually believes China adopts a number of legislation on school bus safety while the *China Daily* story on which this report is based, "*New safety rules for school buses take effect*"[①] uses the plural form of the word "rule" when it actually means a single legislation on school bus safety. In view of this and given the instrumental nature of the Chinese to English translation of soft legal texts for the international communication of China, the conventions in the targeted culture should be followed, as is advocated by legal translation experts (金朝武, 2009).

6. 1. 2 Real Rights Law or Property Law?

Another case of translation error identified in the soft legal texts released by specialized international communication entities of China concerns an important

① http://www.chinadaily.com.cn/cndy/2012-04/11/content_15018627.htm.

legislation in China, namely, *the Property Law of the People's Republic of China* (《中华人民共和国物权法》). Although this law is hailed as a milestone in the legislative history of China, there exists a variety of translations of the very name of this law in the soft foreign publicity texts released by China. For example, while this law is known as *Real Rights Law* when a full translation is released via the magazine *Beijing Review*①, the title of this law is translated into *the Property Law of the People's Republic of China* by www. china. org. cn, a specialized online international communication entity of China. Such inconsistency in the translation of the titles of laws not only may confuse the intended readers, but also may potentially give rise to international legal disputes (刘法公, 2010). In view of this, this author argues that the former translation, namely Real Rights Law, be adopted as the official title of the law, because China follows the German Pandectist system of classification, under which the property law corresponds to the law on real rights. However, since the term "property law" is far more popular in English speaking countries, whose legal systems are based on the common law heritage, the two translations may be used side by side so as to facilitate understanding, provided that the former is used on formal occasions while the latter, namely, property law is used on informal occasions.

6.1.3 Is Mini-Constitution Equal to "小宪法"?

A third case of translation errors in texts released by specialized international communication entities of China are pragmatic in nature. In the article *Major Amendment*, the cover story of the March 22 issue of *Beijing Review*, which focuses on an important amendment to China's Criminal Procedure Law, the author states that "the draft amendment to the law (the Criminal Procedure Law)", also called the "mini-Constitution", took center stage at the Fifth Session of the 11th National People's Congress (NPC) held in Beijing on March 5 – 14. While "mini-Constitution" seems a perfect translation of the Chinese word "小宪法", the implicit information behind the Chinese word will be lost on the English read-

① http://www. bjreview. com. cn/document/txt/2007 – 07/31/content_70969. htm.

ers if it is translated in the present form. The Criminal Procedure Law is called the "mini-Constitution" in China because this Law is secondary only to the Constitution of China in protecting the human rights of citizens①. However, this information is not present in the word-for-word translation "mini-Constitution", because according to the auxiliary texts retrieved through Google, "mini-Constitution" is mostly used to refer to amendments or supplements to Constitutions, or legislation that play a para-constitutional role, such as the Basic Law of the Hong Kong Administrative Region.

This concern for the loss of the implicit information is not unfounded. For example, in an article titled "China improves legal protection for the majority and introduces more control of the few" posted on the Danish Institute for Human Rights, Bjarne Andreasen, Project Manager, and Paul Dalton, Senior Legal Adviser of Danish Institute for Human Rights claimed that the Criminal Procedure Law of China "has the status of a kind of mini-constitution, because China's constitution cannot be applied in court", which, however, is not true, as has been shown above.

Therefore, in view of the instrumental nature of the Chinese to English translation of soft legal texts, of which the article in question is a prime example, it seems better that an explanatory note be added to the sentence: "The draft amendment to the law, also called the 'mini-Constitution' in recognition of its importance in protecting the human rights of citizens."

So far, typical translation errors in the soft legal texts released by entities specializing in the international communication of China have been analyzed and solutions have been proposed according to the translation strategy and tactics identified in the previous chapter. In general, the quality of such soft legal texts is fairly high. However, as will be shown in the following part of this chapter, the performance of Chinese entities engaged in the international communication of China's legal system is far less satisfactory.

---

① http://www.cupl.edu.cn/html/news/col179/2011-09/02/20110902140050074408898_1.html.

6.2 Translation Errors in Texts Released by Concurrent International Communication Entities of China

In spite of the increasing attention to and investment in the efforts to introducing China's legal system, the translation quality is not what it should be. Before going on, let's first look at the following piece of news retrieved from the official website of the Supreme People's Court of the People's Republic of China, which is translated from a law-themed news item titled "深入推进三项重点工作"荣昌杯征文颁奖暨研讨会召开 for the purpose of presenting information on China's legal system:

> Rongchang Cup Writing Competition Awards Ceremony held in Chongqin①
>
> *Beijing, Dec. 3 (Chinacourt. org) 2010 Rongchang Cup Writing Competition Awards Ceremony held in Chongqin, Thursday, December 2, 2010. The writing competition was sponsored by People's Court Daily, Chinacourt. org and Rongchang People's Court. Jing Hanchao, Vice president of the Supreme People's Court attended the awards ceremony and made an important speech.*

In the above brief news item consisting of fewer than 60 words, there are:

One spelling mistake: Chongqin, which should be spelt "Chongqing", which is a city in southwestern China.

At least four cases of violations of punctuation rules (commas between the word "Beijing" and "Dec." in line one, between the words "Chongqin" and "Thursday" in line two and that between the words "Hanchao" and "Vice" in the last line but one should have been followed with a blank space and the word proper name "Supreme People's Court" should have been followed by a comma)

---

① Retrieved from the official website of the Supreme People's Court of the People's Republic of China at http://en. chinacourt. org/public/detail. php? id =4646.

and one violation of capitalization rules ("Vice president" in the last line but one should have been "Vice President", denoting an official title).

At least two cases of grammar errors "held in Chongqin" should have been "was held in Chongqin"; and "Thursday, December 2,2010" in line two should have been "on Thursday, December 2,2010".

At least five points that would have confused even those receivers of the translation who have reasonable knowledge about China, let alone those with little or no knowledge of China: What is the Rongchang Cup Writing Competition? Since Chongqin is clearly a name of place, where is it then? Is it in China or anywhere else? What are the People's Court Daily, Chinacourt. org, Rongchang People's Court and the Supreme People's Court? What is the relation between them?

And finally, the fatal question: Why is a writing competition, which is often associated with literary creation, so relevant to the legal system of China that a court Vice Present actually felt obliged to attend its award ceremony and made an "important"? (for that matter, why is the speech important and in what way?)

All the above errors, mistakes and vague points and seeming irrelevance of the "news item" would have baffled the receiver, and hence foiled the purpose of the translation.

A comparison of the above English translation with the Chinese original of the news item, as is shown below, revealed that translator not only failed to provide necessary information without which the translation would not make any sense at all, but also actually omitted some crucial information in the Chinese original.

"深入推进三项重点工作"荣昌杯征文颁奖暨研讨会召开①

景汉朝出席并讲话

由人民法院报社和重庆市高级人民法院共同主办的"深入推进三项重点工作"主题征文颁奖暨"社会管理的司法创新"研讨

① Retrieved from the official website of the Supreme People's Court at http://rmfyb. chinacourt. org/paper/html/2010 – 12/03/content_19404. htm.

会今天在重庆市荣昌县召开，最高人民法院副院长景汉朝出席会议并就人民法院深入开展三项重点工作作讲话。

When you find out that such inadequately translated text is actually posted under the section of "judicial news" of the official website of the Supreme People's Court of China, the highest court of a jurisdiction with a population of 1.4 billion, you will realize that the Chinese to English translation of soft legal texts for the purpose of presenting China's legal system still leaves much to be desired, which is actually an understatement, as will be found out in subsequent parts of this chapter.

In this section, the top-down functionalist approach to translation problem solving will be put to test. First, the translation type and target text function are determined and a translation brief is formed for each of the three source texts. Then examples of the three types of translation problems and the corresponding translation errors, i. e., failures to solve such translation problems, are identified in the corresponding target texts of the three source texts after a comparison of the source texts and target texts. At last, solutions to the translation problems behind such translation errors are proposed on the basis of the top-down functionalist approach. Since the three target text examples and their corresponding source texts examples are all full-length media reports, they are attached to the book as appendixes while the parts involved in this test of the translation problem solution approach will be quoted in the book proper.

6.2.1 Laying the Foundation: Identification of Target Text Function and Translation Type and Preparation of Translation Brief

The three source texts involved in this part are copied from the section of "Front Page News" (头条新闻) of the official website of the Ministry of Justice of China, while the corresponding three target texts are copied from section 5.1 of the book, "Legal Publicity" (法制宣传) of the English version of the Ministry's website. Then it is clear that the three source texts are intended as "news reports" while the English texts are intended as "legal publicity" materials. Therefore, according to the findings in Section 5. 2. 1, the function of the English texts can be confirmed as informative and appellative and hence the translation involved is instrumental in nature and is part of the efforts to introduce China's legal system to the world.

On the basis of this, a translation brief may be drawn up, which may be shared by the three source texts given their identical functions, addressees, medium used, and time and place, etc.

Translation Brief

Translation purpose: To provide English readers with information on China's legal system and thereby increase their understanding of China and create a favorable environment for the development of China.

Intended target-text functions: Informative and subtly appellative.

The target-text addressees: Those who read English and are interested in China's legal system.

The medium: The Internet.

The time and place for the reception of the target text: Accessible by the Internet from anywhere in the world at any time.

On the basis of the above translation brief, the profiles of the source text and target text are compared and the following findings are made:

Intended functions: Informative and appellative, while the latter function of the source texts is stronger than that of the target texts.

The addressees: the addressees of the source texts are Chinese citizens [the information may be drawn from words like "我国 (our country)", "同志 (comrade)"] with average education or above, with reasonable interest in and knowledge about the legal system of China; the addressees of the target texts are English-users with average education and reasonable interest in China's legal system [otherwise they would not have visited the website (which is not among the first echelon of Chinese entities engaged in external publicity, such as *China Daily*) in the first place] and their knowledge of the Chinese legal system may vary greatly and it is safer to assume that they know very little about China and its legal system（黎信，2009：22）.

The medium: as the same as being on the Internet in both cases.

The time and place: the place is the same, i. e. , any place in the world with access to the Internet; there is some slight difference in time, however, since the translation of the target text may actually take some time. Therefore, some indicators of such difference in time may be necessary.

So far, the following can be inferred on the basis of the above findings and in accordance with the functional approach to solving translation problems:

(1) The instrumental translation should be adopted and therefore, the target text must comply with the conventions and norms of the target culture as indicated in Section 5. 1. 2.

(2) On the pragmatic level, given the possible great disparity between the source text addressees and the target text addressees in knowledge about China and its legal system, it is advisable to change the implicit information that the former may be assumed to have into explicit information, especially presupposed information on China's legal system; and some information that is not closely related to the topic of the source texts may be left out lest the addressees get overwhelmed.

(3) On the language level, the target text should be natural and coherent to the target reader and the bottom-up approach should not be avoided.

In the following three sections, three types of translation errors will be analyzed and solutions be proposed to the translation problems behind them.

6. 2. 2 Pragmatic Translation Errors: Analysis and Solution

Pragmatic translation error 1 (Excerpted from Appendix Ⅵ: Source Text of Example 3 and Appendix Ⅴ: Target Text of Example 3 respectively)

企业如何应对国际金融危机带来的严峻挑战，抓住机遇，实现企业在逆境中发展，努力为中央提出的保增长、保民生、保稳定的大局服务，是每个企业都必须认真思考的重要问题。

Under such circumstances, Chinese enterprises are bound to suffer from severe impacts, thus it is a compulsory course for every corporation to deliberate on how to cope with the daunting challenges and grasp the opportunities in the global financial crisis to rise against adversities and serve the cause of securing growth, livelihood and stability of ***our country.***

As has been pointed out, the relationship between the source text addressees and the source text is different from that between the target text and the addressees thereof, as the former is between compatriots while the latter is between two groups of people who are highly likely to be from different countries, hence the translation "our country" (the underlined part in bold) is inappropriate and should have been changed into "China".

As has been pointed out in the previous section, given the fact that the target text addressees may actually know very little about China, including its legal system, the translator should "step into the shoes" of the addressees, so to speak, and turn the presupposed information in the source text that may be interesting or useful to the target text addressees into explicit information.

Pragmatic translation error 2 (selected from Appendix Ⅱ: Source Text of Example 1 and Appendix Ⅰ: Target Text of Example 1)

司法部副部长郝赤勇在今天召开的全国司法所建设工作会议上强调，加强司法所建设，必须以规范化建设为抓手，内强素质、外树形象，走规范化建设的道路。

Vice Minister of Justice Mr. Hao Chiyong stresses at the National Conference on the Building of Judicial Administrative Stations that the building of judicial administrative stations must center around sandardization in order to strengthen the intrinsic quality and establish the external image.

The Chinese original quoted above is a classical piece of officialese and the English translation thereof literally teems with errors. However, the most important among such errors are pragmatic errors. The receiver of the excerpt from the target text would be baffled by a number of questions: Who is this Vice Minister of Justice? What are judicial administrative stations? Why is the "building" of judicial administrative stations important? It is only natural that they should feel puzzled, because not every Chinese (actually I suspect few) can say with confidence what the main responsibilities of the Ministry of Justice are, or what a judicial administrative station is and what purposes it serves. Such implicit information, therefore, should have been made explicit so that the target text can make sense to the target text receiver and hence achieve its informative function at least.

However, such adjustments should not be overdone or it may lead to new pragmatic and cultural problems. Look at the following excerpts:

Pragmatic translation error 3 (excerpted from Appendixes III and IV respectively)

> 承担着司法行政九项职能的司法所，已成为构建社会主义和谐社会的一支重要力量。

> *The judicial administrative stations who have 9 functions of judicial administration (to guide and participate in People's mediation; to manage, educate and help offenders serving community correction orders by performing the daily duty of community correction; to guide and administer the grass-root legal services; to coordinate the resettlement and reintegration of offenders; to organize and conduct legal publicity and education; to promote grass-root administration in accordance with law by providing opinions and recommendations for governments at the village, township or neighborhood levels to exercise administration in accordance with law; to assist grass-root governments to handle social conflicts and disputes; to participate in the comprehensive administration of public security; and to finish the tasks related with maintaining social stability entrusted by the superior judicial administrative bodies and governments at the village, township or neighborhood levels) have already grown into an important force in building social harmony.*

Clearly, the translator did realize that the presupposed information behind the term "司法行政九项职能 (literally, nine functions of judicial administration)" is important and should therefore be made explicit to the target text receivers. However, he did it in such a way as to cause a cultural translation problem: The excerpts quoted here are actually part of the lead of a news report. By bloating the lead, the translator violated the target culture convention that the lead should be information-rich yet reasonable in length.

To sum up, in the Chinese to English translation for the purpose of the international communication of China, the pragmatic translation problems should and can be identified in advance. By so doing, the translator can properly handle the information offer in the source text by leaving out information not relevant to the text function and adding new information as is necessary for achieving adequacy. However, the translator should remember that he could not do so at the expense of causing new translation problems.

6.2.3 Cultural Translation Errors: Analysis and Solution

As has been pointed out, the three source texts are journalistic texts and hence in instrumental translation, the target texts must conform to the norms and conventions in the target culture. However, the target texts clearly are not translated in accordance with the functionalist approach and the cultural translation problems therein remain basically unsolved.

Cultural translation error 1 (Excerpted from Appendix Ⅱ Source Text of Example 1 and Appendix Ⅰ Target Text of Example 1 respectively)

全国司法所建设工作会议要求以规范化建设为抓手内强素质外树形象。

National Conference on the Building of Judicial Administrative Stations requires the development of intrinsic quality and external image by centering around the construction of standardization.

As has been pointed out in Section 5. 2. 2, the headline of an English news report should be concise yet informative. However, the rumbling "headline" quoted above actually provides very little information on the news report.

Another example of failure to conform to the target culture norms are too lengthy to quote here—paragraphs 5 and 6 of Appendix Ⅵ: Source Text of Example 3 are very long (containing more than 1,000 Chinese characters). Therefore, to conform to the target culture convention that news reports should feature short paragraphs and plain language, the two paragraphs should have been broken down into a number of smaller units, so that the target text would seem more natural.

6. 2. 4 Linguistic Translation Errors: Analysis and Solution

So far, it is clear that all the three target texts quoted here are results of traditional bottom-up translation approaches. Translators adopting such approaches would stick to the source-text structures and ignore the textual functions in the communication situation. As a result, the communication functions: To provide information and in a delicate and subtle way, change the target text receivers' view on China's legal system cannot be achieved.

Linguistic translation error 1 (excerpted from Appendix Ⅲ: Target Text of Example 2 and Appendix Ⅳ: Source Text of Example 2 respectively)

仅以素有**"东方一枝花"**的人民调解工作为例，今年上半年，全国各地司法所指导人民调解组织调解达成书面协议的矛盾纠纷310多万件，调解成功率为96%。

To take People's mediation, with the nickname of ***a unique flower in the east****, as an example, in the first* 6 *months of this year, the judicial administrative stations nationwide guided relevant mediation organizations in* ***successfully solving*** *more than* 3. 1 *million conflicts and disputes through written agreements with a success ratio of* 96% .

The two underlined parts in bold, namely, “东方一枝花” and “a unique flower in the east” seems to be perfectly identical with each on the surface. However, the translation would make the receiver confused: Why is a flower related to “people's mediation” (which is another term that would baffle him)? In what way is it unique? To be sure, many Chinese would have difficulty in identifying the meaning of the Chinese original, which is a metaphor of the People's mediation system of China, a time-honored institution that are flourishing because of the Chinese People's traditional reluctance to go to court. This system, however, has been playing a positive role as a cost-efficient way of solving problems.

Another example of linguistic translation error is “successfully solving” (underlined and in bold type), which is a typical case of word-for-word translation. If something is solved, then it is solved. The adverb then is redundant and should be deleted.

6.3 Summary of This Chapter

In this chapter, translation errors in soft legal texts released by both the specialized and concurrent international communication entities of China are identified from typical texts and are analyzed. It is found that translation errors in the soft legal texts released by the specialized entities are primarily on the pragmatic level, which may be solved by consulting auxiliary texts according to the instrumental translation strategy. The quality of target texts released by concurrent international communication entities is rather poor, and it is found through analysis that in spite of the fact the translation brief calls for an instrumental translation strategy, the translations of soft legal texts released by such concurrent entities are actually carried out on the basis of the documentary translation strategy, in which the linguistic bottom-up approach to solving translation problems is adopted. Consequently, such translations fail to meet the requirements of their translation briefs and therefore fail to achieve the intended translation Skopos.

Chapter Seven Conclusion

So far in the present research, the author has introduced the background and significance of the present research, reviewed the current state of the Chinese to English translation of soft legal texts in the context of international communication of China's legal system and analyzed the Chinese to English translation of soft legal texts in the context of international communication of China's legal system. Upon the findings in the previous five chapters, the author has come to the following conclusions.

7.1 Findings of the Present Research

First, through an overview of the current translation practice for the international communication of China's legal system, it is found out that such practice is extremely unbalanced. The majority of resources and attention have been devoted to the translation of hard legal texts while the translation of soft legal texts, which may reach a far wider readership because they are far less technical and professional in nature, is sadly marginalized. In view of this, the author of the book argues that the role that the translation of soft legal texts play in promoting the legal system of China overseas should be recognized and a fair share of resources and academic attention should be given to it.

Second, the German functionalist approach to translation studies is a viable theoretical framework for studies on the translation for the international communication of China. Through a detailed analysis, it is found in the study that German functionalism fully concords with the rules and principles drawn up by veteran Chinese translators, journalists and other international communication professionals on the basis of their many years of translation practice, and therefore, it is reasonable to say that the German functionalist approach has been directly tested in the translation practice related to China's international communication efforts and that it is a viable theoretical framework for such translation practice.

Third, in view of the Skopos of the Chinese to English translation of soft legal texts for the international communication of China, and the dominant informative function, such translation should be instrumental translation according to the German functionalist approach. Therefore, the information in the source text, including implicit and explicit information, must be properly selected in the translation process and the target text must conform to the cultural norms and conventions and linguistic rules of the target culture.

Fourth, the translation problems in the Chinese to English translation of soft legal texts in the context of international communication of China's legal system are identified as pragmatic translation problems, cultural translation problems and linguistic translation problems in accordance with the German functionalist approach.

Fifth, a top-down functionalist translation approach should be adopted to overcome problems in the Chinese to English translation of soft legal texts in the context of international communication of China's legal system. In this approach the profiles of both the source text and target text must first be properly analyzed and compared according to the translation brief, so as to identify the differences in the communication between the source text producer and the source text addressee from that between the producer and addressee of the target text. In view of such differences, information in the source text should be properly selected and the target text must conform to the cultural conventions and linguistic rules of the target culture. All translation errors, which are failures to properly solve translation problems behind them, may be analyzed and solved to the said top-down functional approach.

7.2 Implications and Limitations of the Present Research

So far, the background and significance of the study on the Chinese to English translation of soft legal texts in the context of international communication of China's legal system has been discussed, and a functionalist solution to the translation problems in such international communication has been proposed and discussed on the basis of a review of the current translation practice. It seems that the present research should draw to a close by now. However, the author believes that some in the findings in the present research may have some useful implications for a number of fields related to the present research.

First, regarding the international communication of China, the author argues that greater attention should be paid to the translation of soft legal texts. Given the bad quality of translations of soft legal texts copied from the websites of the nation's highest judicial bodies, it is high time that the imbalance between hard and soft legal texts in terms of resource and attention received be broken and more efforts be made to improve the translation quality—and ultimately the effectiveness—of the Chinese to English translation of soft legal texts in the context of international communication of China's legal system.

Second, the translator should be empowered. As has been demonstrated by the German functional approach, translators should be designated as a responsible expert of cross-cultural communication, not a humble scribe or bilingual typist. To ensure the realization of the intended functions of the target texts and ultimately the realization of the translation Skopos, the translator should be given greater say in the translation process and be allowed to exercise more flexibility.

Due to the limited time and personal ability, there are still the following limitations in the book, which are listed below as suggestions for further research.

First, the present research is based on a qualitative empirical study. While the types of translation problems are identified and solved using the German functionalist model, a quantitative study is needed to uncover the frequency and distribution pattern of translation problems and translation errors.

Second, the author originally planned to include the translation of hard legal texts as part of the present research; however, due to time limitation, the author had to give up. It is the author's hope that some day there will be an academic research reviewing the translation of hard legal texts and exploring the viability of applying the German functionalist approach to the practice and theory of the translation of hard legal texts.

Third, regarding the imbalance between soft legal texts and hard legal texts in terms of the resource and attention they are given, a research based on modern communication theory may be conducted to reveal the cause of such imbalance and explore the optimal proportion of soft legal texts and hard legal texts translated for the purpose of introducing the legal system of China to the rest of the world.

Appendixes

Appendix Ⅰ: Target Text of Example 1

National Conference on the Building of Judicial Administrative Stations requires the development of intrinsic quality and external image by centering around the construction of standardization[①]

WUHAN, September 10—Vice Minister of Justice Mr. Hao Chiyong stresses at the National Conference on the Building of Judicial Administrative Stations that the building of judicial administrative stations must center around sandardization in order to strengthen the intrinsic quality and establish the external image.

Hao Chiyong points out that currently and in the near future, the building of judicial administrative stations should be strengthened in an all-round way, the organizational structures should be standardized with professional working teams to deliver efficient service through systematic management, and infrastructures should be established in a standard manner so as to enhance the general level of judicial work and make positive contributions to the maintenance of stability, the improvement of People's livelihood and the promotion of social and economic development.

Hao Chiyong requests that judicial administrative organs at all levels should strengthen their efforts in five aspects and strive for five goals in the standardization of judicial administrative stations. First, the efforts in organization building should be redoubled to standardize organizational structures and live up to the demands stipulated by *Several Opinions of Central Committee for Comprehensive Management of Public Security on Further Strengthening the Comprehensive Management of Public Security at Local Levels* jointly issued by the General Office of the CPC Central Committee and the General Office of the State Council, set up

① Retrieved from the English version of the official website of the Ministry of Justice of China at http://www.legalinfo.gov.cn/english/News1/content/2009-11/25/content_1186675.htm? node=7604.

one judicial administrative station for every village and expand the coverage of the services delivered by these stations. Second, the efforts in team building should be strengthened to forge a high quality team of professional cadres featuring firm political beliefs, profound knowledge in the practices, fine working styles and just law enforcement. Third, the efforts in capacity building should be strengthened to deliver more efficient services. Cadres should highlight the study of laws, administrative regulations and policies related to their tasks and responsibilities, grasp relative expertise and knowledge and participate in skill trainings and on-the-job trainings on a regular basis so as to enhance their capacity in solving practical problems, enforcing law in a standardized manner and communicating with the people. Fourth, the efforts in the standardization of management should be strengthened to manage the judicial administrative stations in a systematic manner and make the administration of these stations more standardized. Fifth, the efforts in the construction of infrastructures should be strengthened to build up standard infrastructures. The judicial administrative stations will take the same emblem in order to establish a unified image in various local areas and make it more convenient for the public to seek services as well as for the stations themselves to accept administrative supervision. The working conditions and equipments of the judicial administrative stations should be improved to provide the stations with necessary material guarantee in order to honor their duties and responsibilities.

It is learnt that in recent years, on the basis of multi-research and cautious conclusion, the Ministry of Justice has formed *The Opinion on Strengthening Standardization* (Draft for Discussion). At the conference, centered around the theme of standardization of judicial administrative stations, the participants conducted profound discussions, defined the targets, tasks and working methods of the standardization of judicial administrative stations and reached consensus on major issues.

Discipline Inspection Group Leader to the Ministry of Justice Mr. Han Henglin attended the conference and delivered a speech. He emphasizes that judicial administrative organs at all levels should integrate the Party's guidelines and the decisions and deployments of higher authorities with the practical working situation of the local area, emancipate their minds, seek after truth and hold a down-to-earth attitude, and standardize the judicial administrative stations creatively so as to lay a solid foundation for the grassroots areas and strengthen the capacity of the stations to serve the Party Committee, the government and the people.

(by Correspondents Yu Nayang and Hu Xinqiao and Intern Lin Yan)

Appendix Ⅱ: Source Text of Example 1

全国司法所建设工作会议要求以规范化建设为抓手[①] 内强素质　外树形象

武汉 2009 年 9 月 10 日电　记者于呐洋　胡新桥　见习记者林燕

司法部副部长郝赤勇在今天召开的全国司法所建设工作会议上强调，加强司法所建设，必须以规范化建设为抓手，内强素质、外树形象，走规范化建设的道路。

郝赤勇指出，当前和今后一个时期，要全面加强司法所建设，积极推进司法所组织机构正规化、干部队伍专业化、业务工作效能化、所务管理制度化和基础设施标准化，全面提升司法所工作整体水平，为维护稳定、服务民生，促进经济社会发展作出积极贡献。

郝赤勇要求，各级司法行政机关要着力加强五个方面的工作，努力实现司法所规范化建设"五化"目标：要加强组织建设，努力实现组织机构正规化，认真贯彻中共中央办公厅、国务院办公厅印发的《中央社会治安综合管理委员会关于进一步加强社会治安综合治理基层基础建设的若干意见》，按照一乡一所的设置原则，着力推进司法所组织建设，不断扩大司法所工作覆盖面；要加强队伍建设，努力实现干部队伍专业化，努力造就一支政治坚定、业务精通、作风优良、执法公正的高素质队伍。

要求加强业务建设，努力实现业务工作效能化，重点加强与所承担职能有关的法律法规和政策的学习，熟练掌握相关业务知识和技能，开展经常性技能培训和岗位练兵，不断增强解决实际问题的能力和水平，提高执法规范化水平和群众工作能力；要加强规范管理，努力实现所务管理制度化，不断提高司法所管理工作的制度化、规范化水平；要加强基础设施建设，努力实现基础设施标准化，以树基层统一形象、方便群众办事、便于

---

① Retrieved from of the official website of the Ministry of Justice at http://www.moj.gov.cn/2008ttxw/2009-09/11/content_1152304.htm.

行政监督为目的，统一司法所标示，不断改善司法所办公条件和设施装备，为司法所履行职责提供必要的物质保障。

据悉，近年来，在多次调研和认真总结近年来经验的基础上，司法部形成了《司法部关于加强规范化建设的意见》（讨论稿）。在今天的会议上，与会代表们围绕着司法所规范化建设这一主题，展开了深入的研究讨论，明确了司法所规范化建设的目标、任务和方法，在重大问题上达成了共识。

中纪委驻司法部纪检组组长韩亨林出席了今天的会议并讲话。他强调，各级司法行政机关要坚持把党的路线方针、上级机关的决策部署同本地区工作实际结合起来，坚持解放思想、求真务实，创造性地开展规范化建设工作，切实把基层建强、基础打牢，不断增强司法所服务党委、政府，服务人民群众的功能。

Appendix Ⅲ: Target Text of Example 2

41,000 judicial administrative stations across China resolved more than 3.1 million conflicts and disputes in the first half of 2009①

BEIJING, September 9—The judicial administrative stations who have 9 functions of judicial administration (to guide and participate in People's mediation; to manage, educate and help offenders serving community correction orders by performing the daily duty of community correction; to guide and administer the grass-root legal services; to coordinate the resettlement and reintegration of offenders; to organize and conduct legal publicity and education; to promote grass-root administration in accordance with law by providing opinions and recommendations for governments at the village, township or neighborhood levels to exercise administration in accordance with law; to assist grass-root governments to handle social conflicts and disputes; to participate in the comprehensive administration of public security; and to finish the tasks related with maintaining social stability entrusted by the superior judicial administrative bodies and governments at the village, township or neighborhood levels) have already grown into an important force in building social harmony. To take People's mediation, with the nickname of "a unique flower in the east", as an example, in the first 6 months of this year, the judicial administrative stations nationwide guided relevant mediation organizations in successfully solving more than 3.1 million conflicts and disputes through written agreements with a success ratio of 96% .

These stations are the grass-root bodies of judicial administration at the most basic level, and compose a vital component of grass-root building of political power. At the moment, there are approximately 41,000 established judicial ad-

---

① Retrieved from the official website of the Ministry of Justice of People's Republic of China at http://english.moj.gov.cn/News1/content/2009-11/25/content_1186674.htm? node=7604.

ministrative stations across China with nearly 100,000 employees, among whom 76.5% are college graduates, up by 3 percentage points year on year. Wang Jue, Director General of the Department of Guidance of the Grass-root Work of the Minsitry of Justice, said in an interview with this reporter, "Compared with the past few years, the leadership of the judicial administrative stations has been improved remarkably in terms of education background, knowledge structure and age distribution. A number of young calibers were recruited and they have brought not only vigor and vitality to these stations, but also sustainable talent and intellectual support to the cause of judicial administration".

At present, most of the conflicts, disputes and collective incidents occurred at the grass-root level, and they need to be addressed and resolved on the spot in a timely manner. The judicial administrative stations' duties such as People's mediation, community correction, and education and resettlement of released prisoners are all closely related with solving conflicts and disputes, and safeguarding social stability. Wang Jue pointed out, "In recent years, the workers of these stations have achieved a lot in the neighborhoods of big cities or remote small villages alike through unimaginable hard work and sweat". He also said that these local stations had brought into full play their merits of being close to grassroots and the general public, centering on the focus and serving the overall interests. A number of outstanding station chiefs and other figures such as Yi Mancheng, national model hero of judicial administrative system, have been reported.

It is reported that from 2004 to the end of June 2009, the government accumulatively input 1.7 billion Chinese yuan through national bond resources in 4 batches to set up 24,215 judicial administrative stations, among which nearly 23,000 stations with no fixed office or dilapidated building put up or renovated their offices, and thus finished 94.8% of the planned projects. According to the latest statistics, Jilin, Liaoning, Heilongjiang, Ningxia, Chongqing and Qinghai Provinces (autonomous regions and municipalities) have already completed all their allocated construction projects.

In the past few years, the judicial administrative stations have remarkably improved the working conditions while the station officers have devoted themselves with greater passion to work, conscientiously fulfilling all the duties, and therefore injected vigor into the grass-root work in an all-round way. Since the beginning of this year, when handling traditional civil disputes, these officers have organized various dispute examination and resolution activities, making contribution to maintaining stability, serving People's wellbeing, and promoting steady and relatively rapid economic development.

(by Correspondent Yu Nayang and Intern Lin Yan)

Appendix Ⅳ: Source Text of Example 2

全国4.1万个司法所上半年化解矛盾纠纷310多万件①

北京2009年9月9日讯　记者于呐洋　见习记者林燕

承担着司法行政九项职能的司法所，已成为构建社会主义和谐社会的一支重要力量。仅以素有“东方一枝花”的人民调解工作为例，今年上半年，全国各地司法所指导人民调解组织调解达成书面协议的矛盾纠纷310多万件，调解成功率为96%。

司法所是司法行政工作体系中最基层的组织机构，是基层政权建设的重要组成部分。目前，全国已建司法所近4.1万个，全国司法所工作人员近10万人，具有大专以上文化程度的占76.5%，比去年同期增长3个百分点。“与前些年相比，司法所干部队伍无论是在文化程度、知识结构、年龄结构上都有了明显改善。一大批年轻的高素质人才充实到司法所干部队伍中来，为司法所带来生机与活力，也为司法行政事业发展提供了可持续发展的人才与智力支撑。”司法部基层工作指导司司长王珏今天在接受本报记者采访时说。

当前，各种社会矛盾、纠纷和群体性事件大多发生在基层，需要就地得到及时妥善处理和化解。司法所组织指导和开展的人民调解、社区矫正、帮教安置等工作都与化解矛盾纠纷、维护社会稳定密切相关。“近年来，全国各地无论是城市街道还是偏远乡村的司法所干部都做了大量的工作，付出难以想象的辛劳与汗水。”王珏说，各地司法所发挥贴近基层、贴近群众的优势，围绕中心、服务大局，涌现出全国司法行政系统二级英雄模范易满成等一大批优秀司法所长和先进人物。

据统计，从2004年至2009年6月底，中西部地区国债资金分四批累计投入近17亿元，规划建设司法所24 215个；全国四批累计新建改建无

① Retrieved from the official website of the Ministry of Justice of People's Republic of China at http://www.moj.gov.cn/2008ttxw/2009-09/10/content_1151699.htm.

房、危房司法所近 2.3 万个，完成已下达项目总数的 94.8%。最新统计数据显示，吉林、辽宁、黑龙江、宁夏、重庆和青海六省（区、市）全部完成已下达建设项目。

几年来，各地司法所办公条件在得到明显改善的同时，广大司法所干部以更加饱满的工作热情，认真履行各项职责，全面活跃基层工作，特别是今年以来，他们在化解传统民间纠纷的同时，针对国际金融危机影响引发的各种矛盾纠纷，组织开展多种形式的矛盾纠纷排查化解工作，为维护稳定、服务民生、促进经济平稳较快发展作出了积极贡献。

Appendix V: Target Text of Example 3

Thematic Forum held by Ministry of Justice, Ministry of Commerce and National Popularization of Legal Knowledge Office①

BEIJING, April 29, 2009—Sponsored by Ministry of Justice, Ministry of Commerce and National Popularization of Legal Knowledge Office, supported by Department of Legal Publicity, Ministry of Justice and Legal Daily, the thematic forum "strengthening legal publicity and education among enterprises to actively counter international financial crisis" was held in Beijing today.

It is learned that this thematic forum is an important part of a series of propaganda on implementing " strengthening legal publicity and education among enterprises to actively counter international financial crisis" organized by Ministry of Justice and National Popularization of Legal Knowledge Office with the purpose to implement central government's strategic deployment to promote steady and relatively rapid economic growth, make full use of the legal publicity and education in promoting the social and economic development, and create a favorable legal environment to guarantee economic growth, improve People's livelihood and maintain social stability.

Mr. Zhang Sujun, member of Party Leadership Group, Vice Minister of Justice, Vice Director of National Popularization of Legal Knowledge Office, attended the thematic forum and made a keynote speech. He pointed out that since last year, the global financial crisis triggered by U. S. subprime mortgage crisis has brought extensive and intensive influences to the world economy with scale, scope and severity rarely seen since the Great Depression in the 1930s. Under such circumstances, Chinese enterprises are bound to suffer from severe impacts, thus it is a compulsory course for every corporation to deliberate on how to cope

---

① Retrieved from the official website of the Ministry of Justice of People's Republic of China at http://www.legalinfo.gov.cn/english/news/content/2009-06/08/content_1103031.htm.

with the daunting challenges and grasp the opportunities in the global financial crisis to rise against adversities and serve the cause of securing growth, livelihood and stability of our country.

Zhang Sujun remarked that rule of law is the guarantee while education is the foundation to realize enterprises' sound development and actively deal with the challenges and impacts of the international financial crisis. Therefore, enterprises must enhance their capability to cope with crises in accordance with law, which is also an inevitable choice in market economy in order to deal with all kinds of crises and risks. Legal publicity and education among enterprises has always been one of the priorities in legal education for all, and it is clearly provided in the fifth Five-Year Plan for Legal Popularization that legal publicity and education should be strengthened among enterprise managers so as to improve their ability to run their business according to law. Since the adoption of this plan, many departments and enterprises have deemed legal publicity and education as the foundation in promoting reform and development of the company, taken effective measures to further legal education and have accomplished many achievements.

Zhang Sujun indicated that to properly handle the global financial crisis, legal publicity and education among enterprises must be highlighted and deepened so as to enable employees especially managers to fully understand our country's legal and policy environment for companies and better balance interests and benefits through laws, administrative regulations and policies. In this way, enterprises can walk out of passive positions, shake off difficulties and be revitalized. Leadership in legal publicity should be strengthened and those who in charge should be held responsible for their decisions. Management departments of enterprises at diffent levels should regard legal publicity and education as an important measure to weather the financial crisis. Specialized laws and regulations in the industry and policy measures launched against the crisis should be generalized so as to provide sound service and support for corporation development. Legal publicity and enhancement of legal consciousness and knowledge of employees especially of managers should be put at the top of the agenda. In combination with practical conditions, laws and regulations related to the production, operation and management of enterprises should be popularized in order to strengthen staff members' awareness to prevent risks and run their business in an honest manner according to law, and curb illegal operations which are aimed at short-term returns but might harm the company's long-term development. Laws and regulations on the rights and interests of enterprises and their staff members should be generalized as well to enable them to defend their legitimate rights and interests through legal means. Legal publicity and education departments at all levels should function their role in organization and coordination, promote the campaign of "entry of law into enterprises", strengthen the guidance in legal education activities, suit the realities of different enterprises, and organize well-received outreach campaigns in an effective and efficient manner.

Zhang Sujun stressed that legal publicity and education should be relevant to the production and operation of enterprises, suit the current stage of our economic and social development, focus on the new issues faced by enterprises in the socialist market economy, emphasize the establishment and improvement of modern corporate system, and highlights the challenges imposed on enterprises by the global financial crisis. Targeted campaigns should be organized to better serve the central assignments of companies and provide legal securities for corporation development. The legal education of managers, the major object of the Fifth Five-Year Plan for Legal Popularization, should be prioritized. SOEs must carefully implement *Several Guidelines on Strengthening Enterprise Managers in Studying and Using Law* stipulated by Propaganda Department of the CPC Central Committee, Ministry of Justice, State-owned Assets Supervision and Administration Commission of the State Council and National Popularization of Legal Knowledge Office, organize and improve lectures on law system for leaders and cadres of the enterprise, establish central team law learning system and legal training system, and in accordance with the demand of enterprises' development, stipulate training plans, hold training courses, provide thematic counseling and organize lectures on laws. Besides, we should strengthen legal culture building among enterprises, guide companies to establish legal education bases, open up "law corners", hold a variety of legal education campaigns regularly, and create a favorable environment to study, use and abide by laws. Staff schools, bulletins, columns, internal publications and internet should be deployed to promote legal generalization. Art performance groups should elaborately choreograph legal art programs and perform more frequently and widely. The study and use of laws should be linked to enhance rule of law. Enterprises should start from reality, improve corporate rules and regulations, perfect and standardize operational mechanisms and enhance the level of management according to law.

This forum was hosted by Mr. Xiao Yishun, Director General of Department of Legal Publicity, Ministry of Justice. Mr. Zhou Bingjian, vice president of Legal Daily attended the forum on behalf of the co-organizers. Officials from Department of Treaty and Law of Ministry of Commerce, Department of Laws and Regulations of General Administration of Customs, Zhejiang Provincial Department of Justice, All-China Lawyers Association, State Grid and other enterprises in Beijing and scholars from Renmin University of China have made speeches at the forum. Experts and comrades in charge of legal publicity and education in central state organs, local departments and part of state-owned key enterprises were also present at the forum.

(by reporter Wu Kun)

Appendix Ⅵ：Source Text of Example 3

加强企业法制宣传教育　积极应对国际金融危机[①]
司法部商务部全国普法办举办主题论坛

北京 2009 年 4 月 29 日讯　　记者吴坤

由司法部、商务部、全国普法办公室联合主办，司法部法制宣传司和法制日报社承办的“加强企业法制宣传教育　积极应对国际金融危机”主题论坛今天在京举行。

据了解，此次论坛是落实司法部、全国普法办关于开展“加强企业法制宣传教育　积极应对国际金融危机”主题系列宣传活动的重要内容之一，是为了认真贯彻落实中央关于促进经济平稳较快发展的战略部署，充分发挥法制宣传教育在促进经济社会发展中的积极作用，努力为保增长、保民生、保稳定工作大局营造良好的法治环境。

司法部党组成员、副部长、全国普法办公室副主任张苏军出席论坛并作主旨演讲。他指出，2008 年以来，由美国次贷危机引发的全球金融危机给世界经济发展带来了广泛而深刻的影响，其涉及范围之广、影响程度之深、冲击程度之大，为 20 世纪 30 年代大萧条以来所罕见。在这种形势下，我国企业必将受到一系列的严重冲击。企业如何应对国际金融危机带来的严峻挑战，抓住机遇，实现企业在逆境中发展，努力为中央提出的保增长、保民生、保稳定的大局服务，是每个企业都必须认真思考的重要问题。

张苏军说，实现企业的良性发展，积极应对国际金融危机带来的挑战和冲击，法治是保障，教育是基础，必须努力提高企业依法应对危机的能力，这是市场经济条件下企业应对各种危机和风险的必然选择。加强企业的法制宣传教育一直是全民普法教育的重点之一，党中央、国务院批转的“五五”普法规划明确提出：加强企业经营管理人员法制宣传教育，着力

---

① http://www.legalinfo.gov.cn/index/content/2009-04/30/content_2249009.htm? node=25329.

提高依法经营、依法管理能力。“五五”普法以来，各地、各有关部门和广大企业认真贯彻落实“五五”普法规划，把加强企业法制宣传教育作为推进企业改革、促进企业发展的重要基础工作，不断加大力度，采取多种行之有效的措施，深入推进企业法制宣传教育，取得了显著成效。

张苏军指出，为了妥善应对国际金融危机带来的冲击，必须高度重视加强企业法制宣传教育，通过扎实深入的法制宣传教育使企业员工尤其是经营管理者，充分了解当前我国企业面临的法律和政策环境，充分利用各种法律、法规、政策提供的有利条件，妥善处理各种利益之间的关系，变被动为主动，为企业走出困境注入活力。要切实加强对企业法制宣传教育的领导，按照“谁主管，谁负责”原则，各级企业的主管部门要把加强所属企业的法制宣传教育作为帮助企业应对国际金融危机的重要措施，切实加强对本行业相关专业法律法规和应对国际金融危机相关政策措施的宣传教育，为企业发展提供良好的服务和保障。各类企业要切实把加强法制宣传教育，努力提高企业员工尤其是经营管理者的法律意识和法律素质作为一项重要工作列入工作日程，结合企业的生产经营实际，大力加强与企业生产、经营和管理等各项工作相关的法律法规宣传教育，增强企业全体员工的风险防范意识，强化法治观念，努力做到依法经营、诚信经营，防止为追求短期效益违规违法操作，给企业的长远发展带来危害。要加强维护企业和职工合法权益法律法规的宣传教育，提高企业和职工运用法律手段维护自身合法权益的能力。各级法制宣传教育主管部门，要切实发挥组织协调作用，深入推进“法律进企业”活动，加强对企业法制宣传教育的指导，结合不同类型企业实际，广泛开展适合企业职工喜闻乐见的法制宣传教育活动，不断提高活动的实际效果。

张苏军强调，要紧紧围绕企业的生产经营开展法制宣传教育。企业法制宣传教育必须紧密结合经济社会发展和企业生产经营的实际，围绕在社会主义市场经济条件下企业所面临的新问题，围绕建立和完善现代企业制度，围绕当前国际金融危机给企业带来的一系列挑战，有针对性地开展各种法制教育活动，努力为企业中心工作服务，为企业发展提供良好的法治保障。要重点抓好企业经营管理人员的学法用法。企业经营管理人员是“五五”普法确定的重点对象，国有企业要认真贯彻中宣部、司法部、国资委、全国普法办《关于加强企业经营管理者学法用法工作的若干意见》的要求，建立健全企业领导干部法制讲座制度、中心组学法制度、法律培训制度等，根据企业发展的需要，制订培训计划，采取举办培训班、专题辅导、法制讲座等形式进行培训。要大力推进企业法治文化建设。积极引导企业加强法制宣传教育阵地建设，开辟学法园地，定期开展各种形式的法制宣传教育活动，努力形成企业学法、用法、守法的良好环境。要利用职工学校、墙报、专栏、内刊、网络等阵地开展法制宣传，利用文艺团队，精心编排法制文艺节目，开展法制文艺演出活动，努力增强法制宣传教育的经常性和渗透性。要坚持学法用法相结合，深入开展依法治理活动。各类企业要从实际出发，深入开展依法治企活动，通过健全企业各项规章制度，完善和规范企业运行机制，提高企业法治化管理水平。

司法部法制宣传司司长肖义舜主持论坛。法制日报社副社长周秉键代表承办单位出席论坛。商务部条法司、海关总署政策法规司、浙江省司法厅、全国律师协会、国家电网公司、北京市相关企业的领导和中国人民大学有关专家等在论坛上分别发表演讲。参加论坛的还有部分中央国家机关和地方从事法制宣传教育工作的负责同志、部分中央企业法制宣传教育工作负责同志、有关专家学者以及北京市有关部门和各区（县）法制宣传教育工作负责同志。

Appendix Ⅶ: Chinese and Asian Law Resources[①]

D'Angelo Law Library
University of Chicago Law School
February 2007

中国法律纲

People's Republic of China

Research Contacts

Lyonette Louis-Jacques
Foreign and International Law Librarian
D'Angelo Law Library
(773) 702 - 9612
llou@ midway. uchicago. edu
http://www. lib. uchicago. edu/e/law/

① www. lib. uchicago. edu/e/law/intl/chinese. doc.

Lorna Y. Tang

Associate Law Librarian for Technical Services

D'Angelo Law Library

(773) 702 - 9619

lyt2@ midway. uchicago. edu

http://www. lib. uchicago. edu/e/law/

Bill Alspaugh

Chinese Studies Librarian

Regenstein Library

(773) 702 - 8436

als1@ midway. uchicago. edu

http://www. lib. uchicago. edu/e/easia/

East Asian Collection & Library Staff (University of Chicago, Regenstein Library)

http://www. lib. uchicago. edu/e/easia/

http://ceas. uchicago. edu/people/librarystaff. html

The Center for East Asian Studies (University of Chicago)

http://ceas. uchicago. edu/

East Asian Law Department (University of Washington School of Law, Gallagher Law Library)

http://lib. law. washington. edu/eald/eald. html

The Chinalaw List (formerly the *Chinese Law Net* e-mail list—an electronic discussion group to subscribe to to talk about Chinese law and legal research) (see also Walter Hutchen's Chinese securities law blog at http://www. walter-hutchens. net/blog/)

http://hermes. gwu. edu/archives/chinalaw. html

http://docs. law. gwu. edu/facweb/dclarke/chinalaw/index. htm

Welcome to Chinalaw, an electronic discussion group devoted to issues of modern Chinese law. While it is intended that the law of the People's Republic of China will be the main focus, postings relating to other Chinese jurisdictions or to Chinese legal history are also welcome. All persons with an interest in Chinese law are welcome to subscribe. Current subscribers — numbering 934 as of October 8, 2004 — include business people, law professors, lawyers, and students from many countries.

Legal News Sources & Journal Commentary

BBC Summary of World Broadcasts and Monitoring Reports (in the Asia-Pacific Library, BBCSWB file on LexisNexis) (includes selected Chinese laws in English translation)

Chinese Journal of International Law

http://heinonline.org.proxy.uchicago.edu/HOL/Index?index=journals/chnint&collection=journals

http://chinesejil.oxfordjournals.org.proxy.uchicago.edu/

China Law and Governance Review

http://chinareview.info/

China Law and Practice

http://proquest.umi.com.proxy.uchicago.edu/pqdweb?RQT=318&VName=PQD&clientid=13392&pmid=52143&cfc=1

China Law Blog (China Law for Business)

http://www.chinalawblog.com/

China Law Digest

http://www.chinalawdigest.com/

Chinese Law Prof Blog

http://lawprofessors.typepad.com/china_law_prof_blog/

(includes links to news, discussion fora, research guides, conferences, etc.)

http://docs.law.gwu.edu/facweb/dclarke/public/Research_Guides.html

China Law Reporter

http://www.heinonline.org.proxy.uchicago.edu/HOL/Index?index=journals/china&collection=journals

China Legal Developments Bulletin / Asia Pacific Legal Developments Bulletin

http://www.bakernet.com/BakerNet/Locations/Asia+Pacific/Offices/China/Publications/default.htm

Chinese Law and Government

http://proxy.uchicago.edu/login? url=http://search.ebscohost.com/direct.asp? db=aph&jid=%2226R%22&scope=site

Columbia Journal of Asian Law (formerly the *Journal of Chinese Law*)

http://www.heinonline.org.proxy.uchicago.edu/HOL/Index?index=journals/colas&collection=journals

http://www.columbia.edu/cu/asiaweb/index.html

http://www.columbia.edu/cu/asiaweb/JAL004.htm

Judicial News (in English via ChinaCourt from the Supreme People's Court of PRC)

http://en.chinacourt.org/

Legal Daily Online (in Chinese; up-to-date legal developments in China)

http://www.legaldaily.com.cn/

(other news sources at http://www.law.yale.edu/library/research/china.html#ns)

World News Connection (includes selected Chinese laws in English translation; e-version of the *FBIS Daily Report China*, entire set on microfiche and 1975 – 1996 FBIS Index)

http://wnc.dialog.com/

Zeitschrift für Chinesisches Recht / Newsletter der Deutsch-Chinesischen Juristenvereinigung e. V.

http://www.zchinr.de/

Research Guides

Wei Luo, *Chinese Law and Legal Research* (Buffalo, NY: WU. S. Hein, 2005)

D'Angelo Law Library, Reserve Reading Room XXKNQ47. L86 2005

Thomas H. Reynolds & Arturo A. Flores, *Foreign Law: Current Sources of Codes and Basic Legislation in Jurisdictions of the World* (113-page China section updated 12/2004)

XXK38. R490 1989 D'Angelo Law Library, Reference

http://www.foreignlawguide.com/ (subscription required)

China (links to legal research resources via the AsianLegal Information Institute)

http://www.asianlii.org/resources/214.html

Chinese Legal Research at the University of Washington (William B. McCloy, 2006)

http://lib.law.washington.edu/eald/clr/cres.html

Internet Chinese Legal Research Center (Wei Luo)

http://law.wustl.edu/Chinalaw/

[covers Mainland China (the People's Republic of China or PRC), Taiwan (the Republic of China), and Hong Kong]

Finding Chinese Law on the Internet (Joan Liu, 2005)

http://www.nyulawglobal.org/globalex/China.htm

Web-Based Research Guides on PRC Legal & Business Resources (prepared by Kara Phillips; located at the American Bar Association Section of International Law's China Committee page; includes bibliography of books and articles) (2006)

http://www.abanet.org/intlaw/committees/africa_eurasia/china/bibliography.shtml

Legal System (of the PRC; from the Chinese Ministry of Justice)

http://www.legalinfo.gov.cn/english/LegalKnowledge/LegalKnowledge1.htm

Selected Other Research Guides

Beyond the Border: The Chinese Legal Information System in Cyberspace (Joan Liu, 2001)

http://www.llrx.com/features/china2.htm

A Complete Research Guide to the Laws of the People's Republic of China (Wei Luo & Joan Liu, 2003)

http://www.llrx.com/features/prc.htm

Zhai Jianxiong, *Judicial Information of the People's Republic of China: A Survey* (2002)

http://www.llrx.com/features/chinajudicial.htm

Guide to Law Online: China (Law Library of Congress)

http://www.loc.gov/law/guide/china.html

Internet Guide for Chinese Studies: *Law* (University of Heidelberg)
http://sun.sino.uni-heidelberg.de/igcs/iglaw.htm

China Law Web-Based Resources (Yale Law Library)
http://www.law.yale.edu/library/research/china.html
(covers Mainland China, Hong Kong, and Taiwan)

People's Republic of China (Washburn University Law School)
http://www.washlaw.edu/forint/asia/china.html

Joan Liu & Yu Liying, *Roaming the Virtual Law Library*: *A Guide to Online Sources* (Law Press China: Beijing, 2004)

Nongji Zhang, "Electronic Resources on the Law of the People's Republic of China" (as part of program F – 6, *A Current Appraisal of Chinese*, *Japanese*, *and Korean Legal Research*, 2004 Annual Meeting of the American Association Association of Law Libraries (AALL), Boston, Massachusetts)

Wei Luo, "How to Find the Law of the People's Republic of China: A Research Guide and Selective Annotated Bibliography," 88 *Law Library Journal* 402 – 426 (1996)
http://heinonline.org/HOL/Page?handle=hein.journals/llj88&collection=journals&id=404

Databases

CHINALAWINFO Selected PRC Laws, 1949 – 2005 (database on LexisNexis containing selected PRC cases and legislation in English translation - not up-to-date; the Peking University LawInfoChina database is more up-to-date)

Filename: PRCLEG

http://www.lawinfochina.com/index.asp

iSinoLaw (subscription database including English translations of Chinese legislation)

http://www.isinolaw.com/isinolaw/homepage.htm

Statutes & Codes

CHINALAWINFO Selected PRC Laws, 1949 – 2005 (LexisNexis; English translations)

Filename: PRCLEG

http://www.lawinfochina.com/index.asp

Laws of the People's Republic of China (Asian Legal Information Institute (AsiaLII))

http://www.asianlii.org/cn/legis/cen/laws/

This database contains selected Chinese legislation and related documents that have been translated into English. It includes:

laws, administrative regulations, pronouncements, resolutions, notices, measures,

rules, decisions, decrees, principles, provisions, announcements,

procedures, official replies and circulars (in interim, current and/or planned versions).

The data is from a number of publically accessible sources including the government websites—ChinaLaw (Information Centre for Legislative Affairs Office of the PRC State Council) and ChinaCourt (Supreme Peoples' Court). Many thanks to these organizations for providing this information. Other data will be added as it becomes available. All translations are unofficial.

Ministry of Justice of the PRC (includes new laws and legislative developments and information about the Chinese legal system in English)

http://www.legalinfo.gov.cn/english/englishindex.htm

Supreme People's Court of the PRC (includes links to English-language court news and legal information, and selected PRC laws and regulations in English translation)

http://en.chinacourt.org/

BBC Summary of World Broadcasts and Monitoring Reports (in the Asia-Pacific Library, BBCSWB file on LexisNexis) (includes selected Chinese laws in English translation)

World News Connection (includes selected Chinese laws in English translation; e-version of the FBIS *Daily Report China* available on microfiche at Regenstein Library at microfcDS 23; see also the Electronic Index to the 1975 – 1996 FBIS *Daily Report China*)

http://wnc.dialog.com/

The Laws of the People's Republic of China (Beijing: Foreign Languages Press, 1987 –)

(available from DePaul, John Marshall, Loyola, UIC-request via CLAS/ILL)

Laws and Regulations of the People's Republic of China (Beijing: China Legal Pub. House, 2001 –) (available via ILL) (16v. looseleaf including "English translations and Chinese text of all commercial and public legislation at the national level" of interest to business: v. 1. Contents—v. 2. Constitutional law—v. 3. Civil and commercial law—v. 4 – 5. Administrative law—v. 6 – 13. Economic law—v. 14. Social law—v. 15. Criminal law—v. 16. Litigation procedures and non-litigation procedures).